now is *gone*

now is *gone*

GEOFF LIVINGSTON
WITH BRIAN SOLIS

Bartleby Press
Baltimore • Washington

Bartleby Press
9045 Maier Road
Laurel, MD 20723
800-953-9929
www.BartlebythePublisher.com

ISBN: 9780910155731
Library of Congress Control Number: 2007937209

Printed in the United States of America

Contents

Todd Defren: Social Media Releases

Brian Oberkirch: Insights That Matter

Laura Ries: New Media

Kami Watson Huyse: Social Network Overtones

Scott Baradell: New Thicket

Acknowledgements

I know acknowledgements can be boring, but if you ever write a book, you'll know they are necessary. Such a process represents a major, time-consuming endeavor that requires help.

A special thank you to my wife, Caitlin, who tolerated this intrusion into our lives for three months.

Thank you to Brian Solis who kept my aim true during the drafting and conceptualization process. You didn't even know me, yet you participated. Truly, you demonstrated the spirit of social media.

My research assistant, Andrew Waber, deserves a special thank you for researching, writing a couple of case studies, and drafting the chapter summaries. Well done, Andrew.

Thanks to Michele Capots, Cynthia de Lorenzi, publisher Jeremy Kay, and Jen Sterling for keeping me going.

Special thanks to Scott Baradell, Paula Berg, Toby Bloomberg, Todd Defren, Shel Holtz, Kami Watson Huyse, Brian Lusk and David Meerman Scott for going the extra mile. You are great sources!

To all the bloggers and sources cited, this is your wisdom, not mine. Thank you. Hopefully, we made a difference for some people with this effort. And hopefully, we have honored the wisdom you shared, either directly or through your writings.

Seven Categories of Social Media

Kami Watson Huyse*

1) Publishing Platforms: These consist of platforms and tools that allow the author(s) to set the content of the initial offering. Most offer a way for others to comment on the content and include RSS feeds to syndicate the copy

- Examples: Blogs, Podcasts and Vlogs or Video Blogs

2) Social Networking Sites: These sites allow users to interface by becoming friends and/or sharing favorites. They allow the individual user to have their own space, while also incorporating links and other connections to other users

- Examples: YouTube, LinkedIn, Twitter, Flickr, MySpace, and Facebook

3) Democratized Content Networks: These sites allow all

---

* Republished with premission

users to contribute equally, usually with some sort of ability to vote for the best content, or to override, in the case of Wikis, previously submitted content.

- Examples: Digg, NewPR, Wikipedia and old-fashioned forums of all kinds

4) Virtual Networking Platforms: These often require third-party interfaces to participate (though some can be accessed through the browser), and consist of a virtual reality experience with other users.

- Examples: Second Life and There.com

5) Information Aggregators: These are publicly available, machine driven aggregators of niche content, usually with some human editing (such as adding RSS feeds) involved in the process.

- Examples: Techmeme and Power 150 Kitchen Sink

6) Edited Social News Platforms: These are sites where users recommend links and can make comments on the stories that make it through the human editors.

- Examples: Fark and Spin Thicket

7) Content Distribution Sites: Sites that allow the user create, collect and/or share content and distribute by providing RSS, code and/or e-mail options. Widgets would also fall into this category.

- Examples: Scrapblog, Del.icio.us and Clearspring[1]

---

[1] Kami Huyse, "If the Shoe Fits," Communications Overtones, April 25, 2007 (http://overtonecomm.blogspot.com/2007/04/join-network-of-networks.html).

Introduction

Brian Solis

Author of *PR 2.0* and *Principal of Futureworks*

Is the idea that public relations needs to improve evolutionary or revolutionary?

Evolutionary, of course.

How about the fact that technology has completely changed the tools we use to communicate our messages?

Again, evolutionary.

How about that in order to succeed in the future of marketing, we need to think less about pitching and instead better understand the dynamics of sociology to engage in conversations with media as well as customers directly?

This concept is revolutionary—although common sense would tell us that it should have been there all along. But it wasn't, and it needs to be.

The good news is that it is already in practice among the edglings who are proving its potential and showcasing the benefits of what is referred to as participatory and conversational marketing. This will completely change how we think about and approach communications. These are a few of the philosophies driving the renaissance of PR.

PR is The Ugly Duckling of Marketing

Public Relations is the most misunderstood and undervalued art in marketing communications. Company executives don't understand it, and as a result can't appreciate it. And PR, as an industry, hasn't done the best job of PR for itself, leaving the sector stale and second-class.

While advertising is a creative process, Web marketing is function of science, direct marketing is driven by recipes, investor relations is governed by laws and regulations, and event marketing is a luxury for branding and lead generation, PR is the bastard sibling to all of the above.

Everyone claims to understand its value, but the entire art and science of PR is often oversimplified to the point of absurdity—and for the less marketing savvy executives, it is often confused with and compared to the immediacy of advertising.

Here's an inane, yet typical underestimation of the PR process:

Let's say a company has news. First, we write a press release and fill it with jargon, adjectives, more information than anyone could possible interpret and digest, add fake quotes, and spin the hell out of it for good measure. Then we send it to our top reporters and place it on the wire. Within moments, we're asked about the status of coverage in *The Wall Street Journal, Business Week, USA Today*, etc.

This isn't PR. This is a real-world assessment and expectation by many company executives who think that by simply following a process of creating and distributing news, that top influencers will stop what they're doing just to cover the story.

It's almost like buying a paint by numbers masterpiece, following the instructions, and expecting it to be displayed in a museum of modern art—because, hey, you painted it.

PR is not about following steps. Nor is having news a guaranteed mechanism for publicity or an excuse for PR to hide behind a mechanical process. Yes, there are processes. Yes, there should be metrics. Yes, there should be press coverage. However, the role of PR in any company should be reviewed and agreed upon before it's deployed and measured.

PR doesn't stand for Press Release or Publicity Regime. It stands for Public Relations, and everything about it up until now is broken.

From the way company executives expect PR to perform and how it is supported, to the way PR agencies structure their billing and services, from the spin we use to hide our lack of understanding and/or passion, to the spam that is blasted to reporters everywhere hoping to land enough press coverage to justify our existence, PR has become a mechanical process aimed at appeasing company executives rather than the people who are looking for real news and information.

PR is about people, and people are different. They expect to receive information in a way specific to themselves.

The bottom line is that we used to rely on certain influencers (beacons that can transmit information to targeted or wide groups of people, and in doing so, shape the public perception along the way) to carry our news to our target audiences, and their readers—a collection of our desired market demographics—relied on those purveyors to show them what was new and to verify or deconstruct the product's claims.

That was Then, This is Now

You're here because you realize that there's something more, and this book is written for you. You are a marketing professional and you want to improve your game. Or, you are a savvy company leader who wants to make the right decisions for the right reasons on how to cultivate relationships with the public, from reporters and analysts to intermediaries and customers.

The landscape for collecting and sharing news is changing, and it's going to push PR out from behind the curtain into the spotlight.

This book is intended to bring the conversation of the new world of PR directly to you. No need to subscribe to weekly industry rags, read hundreds of blog posts, or hire consultants to open your eyes. Here you will find vision, wisdom, and reports from the field to help you grow, communicate naturally, and improve your company's marketing process.

The conversation about the value of PR is more relevant and important now than ever before. Over the last ten years, new technologies were introduced that set in place changes that are forcing the evolution of PR and changing the face of corporate communications.

Web 1.0: The Spark that Altered the Future

New PR started with Web 1.0 and the explosion of Internet

media. It was a whole new world and it fundamentally changed our lifestyle and popular culture.

Traditional media expanded its presence from print to the Web. But more importantly, it presented a much more accessible and expansive channel for people to be heard.

It was about content and e-commerce.

Suddenly everyone could build a Website, post content to other online networks, or join and participate in online forums, groups, and communities (way beyond the original Bulletin Board System), where people could converge around interests and topics to share information and spark conversations.

The Web was now the stage for enthusiasts to capture a global audience in ways that traditional citizen journalism, pirate radio, and public access television never could.

New technology drove commercial recognition of the original "meet-ups," with real-world user groups forming all over the world to discuss and review the latest technology, applications, and services that benefited particular professions and lifestyles—all facilitated by the Web.

Enter the *real* introduction of marketing, PR, advertising, and all monikers "2.0."

Yes, the Web changed everything over ten years ago! It flipped the entire industry on its head and gave birth to an entirely new and constantly evolving network of global online media channels that spawned new communications tools and approaches. It made tech cool. It also created a new set of influencers, and ultimately inspired a new market for a higher caliber of communicators.

It was the beginning of the end of one-way, and methodic

PR, and the beginning of true "public" relations. For the first time, elitist, fringe marketers were discovering and figuring out how to cultivate the new set of global microcommunities, all strung together by the World Wide Web.

PR 2.0: The New School of Communications

PR 2.0 represents change in our approach and thinking. It is not just a trendy moniker. Eventually it all gets folded back into plain PR, but for now, the ideas of PR 2.0 are so different that they need to be examined and understood separately.

This is the dawn of PR 2.0—my focus and my passion. With it, PR has an opportunity to reinvent itself, becoming the pillar of support for all marketing communications.

When I first started using the term in the mid-90s, I didn't realize just how radically and quickly the Web would pull a ctrl-alt-del on the entire PR game. What I did know, however, was that PR and marketing would never be the same. This would allow communications professionals to rebuild direct relations with the public.

Web 1.0 gave a voice to that public, allowing anybody who knew how to use HTML or was determined enough to learn the software for DIY Web sites to participate on boards and interact within online groups. It was the end of broadcast, the beginning of community interaction, and the reinvigoration of relationships.

PR 2.0 was coined to document the renaissance of communications, not to capitalize on trends or disregard all the milestones of the last 100 years of media evolution, which are many. Now, more than ever, a poignant intersection of PR and technology is exposing PR's weaknesses and causing a Darwinist evolution that may force many old school PR people out of work.

What is most interesting is that it took ten years to bring the ideas and philosophies of PR 2.0 into the public forum.

Why PR 2.0 Now?

After the dotcom bust of Web 1.0, tech architects went back to the drawing board. In doing so, they created a new underlying fabric that would transform the Web from a mostly one-way street into a fully interactive and portable medium.

Without arguing over the semantics of what Web 2.0 is or isn't, it is undeniably responsible for expediting PR's need to evolve. Web 2.0 is dynamic, driven by the wisdom of the crowds and user generated content via contribution, participation, and sharing information online.

The term "Web 2.0" was coined by Tim O'Reilly, who describes it this way:

> Web 2.0 is the business revolution in the computer industry caused by the move to the Internet as [a] platform, and an attempt to understand the rules for success on that new platform. Chief among those rules is this: Build applications that harness network effects to get better, the more people use them. (This is what I've elsewhere called "harnessing collective intelligence.")

In a sense, the Web was now "socialized." It took the mass appeal of Web 2.0 and the introduction of these rapidly emerging social tools and platforms to get the "early market majority" to see and evangelize the prospects of new PR.

The difference between Web 1.0 and now is the new inter-

Web 1.0	Web 2.0
DoubleClick	—> Google AdSense
Ofoto	—> Flickr
Akamai	—> BitTorrent
mp3.com	—> Napster
Britannica Online	—> Wikipedia
personal websites	—> Blogging
evite	—> upcoming.org and EVDBs
domain name speculation	—> search engine optimization
page views	—> cost per click
screen scraping	—> web services
publishing	—> participation
content management systems	—> Wikis
directories (taxonomy)	—> tagging ("folksonomy")
stickiness	—> syndication

active foundation that has created a frenzy around the socialization of, and interaction with, content created, read, and shared by you and me, as well as traditional media. This is the social media revolution, and it is defined by interactive publishing, broadcast, discovery, and search channels that make all of this content available to the masses. It changes the entire game of PR and marketing communications for the better.

PR 1.0 was all about controlling the message and broadcasting it.

PR 2.0 embraces transparency and enables stakeholders in the company, its team, and its place in the market, now and in the future. It encourages participation in online networks and communities in order to spark conversations to help people solve problems and discover new solutions.

PR 2.0 and Social Media

Social media is a product of Web 1.0 and Web 2.0. It is the democratization and socialization of information as well as the tools to facilitate online conversations. To put it another way, it is the shift from one-way to two-way conversations.

Monologue has transformed into dialog.

Social tools such as blogs, social networks, social bookmarks, podcasts, livecasts, virtual worlds, news aggregators, microblogs, online video, and all forms of user generated content and the ecosystems that support them are creating a global neighborhood of peer-to-peer influence, (footnote coined by Shel Israel). But, let me repeat, *but*, this new realm of online interactivity will not tolerate marketers, nor does it wish to be marketed to.

These networks are active, vibrant, and flourishing because social media has democratized the Web, and we the people are producing, sharing, and conversing in and around traditional media—without being governed by editors or moderators.

Social media is the one of the most important ingredients in PR 2.0. People now have a completely different routine and process for reading, interacting with, and sharing information. The other ingredients for PR 2.0 include listening, reading, transparency, participation, and understanding people's needs and the unique channels that reach them.

The evolution of social media is also forcing the most dramatic transformation in PR and corporate communications to date. Now is gone, and it's time to engage or find a new career.

This is our chance to not only work with traditional journalists, but engage directly with a new set of accidental influencers, also known as enthusiasts or citizen journalists. We can talk with customers, now also content producers, directly.

Social media is exposing PR's weaknesses and calling for reform. Why?

- We don't get it
- We're gatekeepers
- We're spammers
- We sell snake oil
- We rival politicians' slippery answers to tough questions
- We love adjectives and speak in messages
- Metrics: We don't need no stinking metrics!

But that's why you have this book.

This is about changing along *with* media.

No bullshit. No hype. Just an understanding of markets, people's needs, and how to reach them at the street level— without insulting everyone along the way.

The best PR pros read publications and understand who they want to reach and why before pitching an idea. That's not PR 2.0, but it certainly isn't commonplace in general PR today.

With the advent of PR 2.0, we must now act and practice relations by combining sociology with the tools currently available for transparent conversations. We have to be part of the communities in which we wish to participate, and in order to do that, we must act as patrons first, never as overzealous marketers. Without transparency and understanding, we won't be invited back to the conversations that are taking place without us.

This is about humanizing our companies and their benefits so that people care about what we're saying. Forget loyalty, forget transactions, and screw brand resonance. Without the ability to humanize our story and communicate with people in the places they go for information, how can we expect them to care, let alone buy anything?

PR 2.0 makes you listen, watch, think, and then participate. It makes you smarter. It makes you more sincere. This is public relations, and the public has the ability to listen and expose your disingenuousness.

PR 2.0 in the Social Economy

Web 2.0, PR 2.0, and social media aside, this is more about sociology than the tools to facilitate new PR. This is about creating a new breed of communications professionals for a new century. This is about change.

Tools will evolve. People generally stay the same. It's human nature.

As stated, social media has created a new layer of influencers that expands companies' ability to expand their customer service and focus. It is the understanding of the role the public plays in the process of not only reading and disseminating information, but sharing and creating content for others to experience. This, and only this, will allow us to truly grasp the future of communications.

The socialization of information and the tools that enable it are the undercurrent of social media and ultimately the social economy.

Content is the currency of that economy, and acts as the new democracy by which we, the people, are ensuring that our voices are heard. New PR is a mashup of new and traditional media that spans across advertising, PR, customer service, marcom, sales, and community relations.

With the injection of social tools into the mix, people now have the ability to impact and influence the decisions of their peers and other newsmakers. The wisdom of the crowds is creating diverse markets that drive microeconomies and dedicated ecosystems that are defining the social economy.

If you want to survive in this economy, you can't just sit on the sidelines. Those who participate genuinely will succeed; everyone else will either have to catch up or miss the game altogether.

PR 2.0 starts with listening and reading, and leads to insight, understanding, and perspective. This inspires respect, which is the critical ante for participation in the social economy.

Listening is marketing.
Participation is marketing.
Media is marketing.
Conversations are marketing.

These are pretty powerful statements, and they are the essence of the future of marketing. Together, they combine the ability to succeed in dynamic relationships with multiple markets.

Markets are Conversations

Conversations are driving the new social economy. They are active in every industry at every level, from businesses to consumers, and in many cases they're about you and/or your competitors.

These markets create and influence transactions and behavior.

Participating here is not optional. How effectively you participate will determine the success or failure of your company in the long term.

The most common mistake marketers make is confusing markets with audiences instead of finding the specific horizontal and vertical markets and the people that collectively represent them. These are people who can benefit from your products, but don't respond to spam or traditional broadcast, us vs. them PR. They want to hear what you can do for them as it relates to their specific market demographic. They do not want to hear marketing-speak or messages. Instead, they want to hear the benefits specific to their community.

Messages are not conversations. This is where most companies and PR people fall down. People just don't communicate that way.

As Doc Searls once said, "There is no market for messages." Here's an example:

Hi, my name is Brian and I'm an innovative, captivating, and visionary person who is trying to revolutionize the world of communications so that the industry can monitor the evolutionary paradigm shift occurring as the democratization of information and user-generated content spans across the chasm, while riding the cluetrain, influencing early adopters, energizing the market majority, and engaging the global microcommunities that define the long tail in this Web 2.0 world.

Markets are not comprised of audiences.

Conversations are the roads between companies and customers, and with the right marketing, those roads will always lead back instead of to the competition. In one sense, PR 2.0 is the new customer service, fusing marcom, PR, and customer relations all in one department.

Everything we're integrating into the marketing mix is aimed at sparking and cultivating not only conversations, but relationships. It's about humanizing companies and their products and services so that they matter to people.

Jay Rosen's great essay "We are the People Formally Known as the Audience" introduced an entirely new concept of reaching people that ultimately influenced marketing. Marketing and PR have always looked at markets as audiences instead of acknowledging and approaching the various groups of people that were, as I interpret it, "formerly" known as the audience. This is why most PR people feel that one press release is the magic net that can coral the masses.

However, in order to reach people, we have to figure out who they are and where they go for information. You'll quickly discover that a magic net doesn't exist.

Conversations are taking place within communities all

over the world, united by common interests and passions. These communities and conversations are the new markets, and PR 2.0 is about reaching them directly with benefits and solutions (whether it's about your product or a topic inside your experience.)

The best communications programs will reach out eventually to traditional media, bloggers, consumers, and communities—from A-listers down to the long tail. But this will require a new mindset.

This is about speaking with, not "to" or "at" people.

These concepts define how to participate in what's referred to as the Long Tail and the new regime of influencers in the micromedia.

Parting Thoughts

The principles of PR 2.0 are a collective set of discussions about how to practice PR in the social economy. These philosophies and methodologies explore how to do PR in a way that works in a conversational medium without demeaning the intelligence of everyone involved. It's also about improving PR and restoring value and respect to the PR industry.

The new world of media is a sea full of sharks—most of whom would love nothing more than to have PR pros for breakfast, lunch, and dinner. But our survival and success is the future of integrated communications.

The future of marketing integrates traditional and social tools, connected by successful, ongoing relationships with media, influencers, and people.

Remember, the future of communications lies in introducing sociology to marketing strategy. Technology is just technology. The tools will change. The networks will evolve. Mediums for distributing content will grow.

As you participate in each of these new discussions, the key ingredient to ensuring transparency is realizing that whatever you do is less about the company, per se, and more about how your customers can succeed in their business or how people can simply improve their personal lives. They learn. You learn. It's about building a community around them—literally. The rest are just tools to facilitate the conversation.

Let's not forget that traditional print, online, and broadcast all remain relevant media today. With the new PR mindset, they will all benefit from the real-world intelligence and street smarts garnered by, and from, those who engage.

We, the people, in order to form a more perfect union, will democratize the Web so that our voices will be heard and markets will shift in directions that benefit us as consumers and producers.

By listening, reading, and participating, corporate marketing will become smarter and more approachable than ever before. This is how we humanize brands, create loyalty, and earn customers' business.

The best companies will let go of their message and control of gatekeeping in social realms and trust their employees to carry them forward. Don't get me wrong, traditional marketing can still run as it has; it just now needs a more complementary partnership and a more open and genuine mindset in order to integrate with all new media activities. You must achieve a better understanding of the people who comprise the markets you're trying to reach along with their needs, pains, options, and, where they go for information. Put some service back in customer service and put some relationships back into public relations.

In the world of social media, companies will earn the community of customers they deserve.

The PR revolution will be socialized. Engage or die.

Chapter 1
A Moment of Clarity

I n life there are very few moments of clarity when you realize that things have completely changed. These moments vary in cause and significance. They might be intensely personal, like the birth of a child, or they might affect our entire nation or even the world, such as the assassination of a president. Other less momentous but still important events might be a mentor's unexpected departure or even the emergence of a new technology like high-definition television.

For me, one of those moments occurred when Jim Webb won the Virginia senatorial race in November of 2006. He had done the impossible in defeating George Allen, a formidable opponent who only three months earlier was considered a serious 2008 presidential GOP candidate. George

Allen was considered so safe for re-election that his initial campaign manager left to work on a race that was considered tougher. Allen was already visiting early GOP presidential primary states in anticipation of an expected 2008 bid for the GOP presidential nomination.[1]

During the campaign, Allen publicly called someone who was filming his event "macaca." This began to be perceived as a racial slur, and the Webb campaign intentionally spread the news through social media outlets like blogs and YouTube. The ensuing uproar in the media and back again into the blogosphere turned a runaway race into a dogfight, and ultimately it cost the Republicans control of the Senate.[2]

When the election was declared for Webb, I knew the face of communications had changed forever. As a practicing PR pro of fourteen years, the Webb victory caused me to entirely rethink my approach to public relations and marketing. What was fun and experimental became the primary thrust of my business. The world changed for me.

Social media—blogs, social networks, localized search enabled maps, SEO, user generated video and audio—had arisen with millions upon millions of content producers. These many content creators and readers had suddenly achieved a new level of power and weight. We could change the way countries were run with one major initiative.

At that point, it was time to stop experimenting with new media and get to know everything possible about it. The social media boom was different from the dot-com era, with users fueling new media, not venture capital-backed start-ups. As a result, the trend continues to grow in scope, scale, and impact. Communications has evolved more in the last ten years than it has in the previous 100.

Consider how much more powerful social media forms have become compared to traditional Web powerhouses. "2006 was the year when the programmable Web eclipsed the static Web every time: flickr beat Webshots; Wikipedia beat Britannica; Blogger beat CNN; Epinions beat Consumer-Reports; Upcoming beat evite; Google Maps beat MapQuest; MySpace beat friendster; and craigslist beat Monster," write *Wikinomics* authors Don Tapscott and Anthony Williams.[3]

Many executives throughout the country have awoken to the increasing power of social media, and they want to know how to engage in this dynamic new environment. Now there's an incredible amount of user-generated information, content, and entertainment streaming throughout the world's networks. The wires, cables, and airwaves are atwitter. At the same time, the environment seems to be dangerous, with users and networks flaming companies who try to sell to them, or worse, have public problems like JetBlue's mass stranding of passengers over Valentine's Day, 2007.[4]

Given the complexity of the situation, the newness of the technologies, and the dangers of a flawed strategy, executives find themselves in a sudden quandary. They must determine how to get their company or organization successfully engaged in social media, and quickly. Yet social media successes are not created overnight, with many current top brands and networks evolving over months and years.

This book provides organizations and executives with a foundation to help create social media strategies for their companies. It does not teach would-be bloggers best practices, or tactical line managers the best way to execute a podcast or a blog post. There are many books that cover the actual day-to-day marketing activities in the social media world.[5] Instead, this book will discuss the general strategic principles and major aspects of social network marketing, providing executives a primer to begin their effort.

The rest of this chapter discusses the general trends driving social media and their impact on business. Ensuing chapters discuss whether or not a company really is ready for social media; keys to creating great content; outbound marketing in the social media world; and integrating social media into an organization's overall marketing effort as well as the impact on larger marketing and public relations departments' means and methods. Finally, our primer closes with a series of interviews conducted on my Buzz Bin Blog with some of the most brilliant minds in social media marketing today.

The Migration to Social Media

The following will frame our discussion about social media:

- Migration to social media
- Social media's impact on businesses
- The great challenge for businesses

With more choices and much more content, media usage patterns have shifted. Generation X, Generation Y, and the following generations are increasingly digital, leaving behind cable TV and print newspapers in favor of text messaging, Facebook, YouTube, and Digg! Now, instead of relying on the integrity of a newspaper's movie review or car featured in a magazine, potential buyers can go online and read actual consumers' opinions based on practical experience.

Social media users are no longer beholden to one voice (often influenced by corporate marketing and PR machines), or a limited network of friends. It is peer-to-peer marketing at its finest, turbocharged by the viral nature of what Doc Searl calls today's Live Web.[6] Our culture is evolving from reactive to proactive with every new participant in the many realms of social media.

A world of experiences lie at consumers' fingertips, and many simply go to Google (or Yahoo!, MSN, Ask! or Technorati) to begin their search for information. When they search, social media sources are often listed as top content vehicles. The result has challenged corporate outreach campaigns, providing disruptive feedback that counters their marketing and public relations efforts.

Social Media Success Story:
The Red Cross Uses Social Media for Crisis Situations

Ike Pigott, Communications Director of the Red Cross' Southeast division, is responsible for disaster operations in Alabama, Mississippi, Florida, North and South Carolina, Georgia, and Tennessee. Before taking on his current role, Ike was working for the Birmingham Area Chapter during Hurricane Katrina. At that time, the Birmingham, Alabama chapter's call volume from local media, local individuals, groups seeking to donate items, and clients who were looking for service, was so high that Ike couldn't keep up with it all.[7]

The inability to field calls presented a problem for the Red Cross, particularly in the Southeast region, which is habitually hit by the most severe weather this nation has to offer in hurricanes and tornadoes. The traditional phone, fax, and press release system could not scale up to handle the increased need for communication intermediaries during a catastrophic event such as Katrina. As such, it couldn't provide quick, useful, and reliable communication to affected people during a disastrous event.[8]

Knowing social media could offer a solution, Ike started to blog, and though some media took to it, he had not found the correct method for information dissemination. While blogs had been used in Birmingham with some success, Ike decided to add short (thirty to forty second), quickly and easily made podcasts that simply gave an audio version of their news releases. The media—radio in particular—loved the podcasts, using them in their telecasts.[9]

The Red Cross Regional Communications Director at this time, Laura Howe, saw this as the best part of this new social media initiative. As she moved up to Director of Disaster Public Affairs, she became a social media evangelist, spreading the best practices from Ike's experiments throughout the Red Cross. Ike was also promoted to Regional Communications Director.[10]

Using social media, Red Cross representatives were able to get disaster pages up for the Alabama and Georgia areas affected by a set of tornadoes within thirty minutes of landing at the Birmingham airport. Populating information remotely enables the Red Cross to recruit volunteers from anywhere to be a poster of disaster-related information on the Web. Using this system, a local Red Cross office that may be without power could still phone a volunteer blogger and tell him or her to post vital information on a disaster news page, which would be quickly picked up by the media. Blog comments are turned off due to the inability to field them during a crisis.[11]

With widespread Internet connectivity in the United States, this method reaches more people quickly and efficiently. Similar programs with podcasts and "disaster newsroom blogs" have been used in Oklahoma, Alabama, Georgia, Florida, Texas, Kansas, and even in northern states struck by a Nor'easter.[12]

The Red Cross has not abandoned faxing or other types of communication, but prefers using social media for disaster relief purposes. Ike and other Red Cross media specialists target the media and the public with these social media initiatives. Because of this method's success, other regional communications directors have embraced the relative simplicity of blog, podcast, and RSS feed outreach within a preexisting, well-supported network.[13]

"This success has accelerated our adoption of proactive social media in other venues," said Ike. "We have [had] several successful incidents where we've spotted a burgeoning complaint on a blog, and have taken the appropriate measures to either correct a wrong impression or repair a relationship with the writer and the Red Cross. This has also provided a new means of volunteering, which is essential for our recruitment of youth. There are millions of high school and college kids who are living in a social media world. Giving them an opportunity to take what they know and support the Red Cross will reap big dividends."[14]

With the rise of social networks, consumer trust in traditional media forms has dramatically declined. The public no longer wholeheartedly believes in reporters now that there are alternative voices to read and verify contemporary newspaper stories. This encourages independent voices and criticisms.

On April 16, 2007, *BusinessWeek* wrote, "Trashing brands online can also be high theater.[17] Rats cruising around a Greenwich Village KFC/Taco Bell on YouTube.[18] MySpacers busting their employers' chops. Faux ads bashing the Chevy Tahoe as a gas-guzzling, global-warming monster.[19] Millions of people watch this stuff—then join in and pile on. Is it any wonder companies lose control of the conversation?"

Origin of Brands author Laura Ries commented on the impact social networks have on brands in such situations: "As quickly and as easily as PR can build a brand, PR can take a brand down. Negative PR is incredibly damaging. And with the growth of new media, mainly the Internet, it can happen faster than ever. Look no further than Don Imus, JetBlue, or Taco Bell for proof of this fact…non-famous people or brands can be annihilated by even mild scandals. If you're not famous, you seldom get a second chance."[20]

How far will the pendulum swing? Already people accept that negative commenting and rumors on blogs may not be accurate, thanks to a faux scandal about Apple. Regardless, businesses are realizing they will be forced to communicate to their customers in the comsumers' own preferred social media forms. Instead of businesses trying to find customers, this time businesses are trying to play catch-up with their customers.

Of course, this fear represents only a very small part of the story. Businesses that leverage social media intelligently have great things to gain from new media, including positive conversations with customers, better communications, buyers who consider the company part of their community, increased brand loyalty, longer relationships, and much, much more.

One of the original and most respected marketing bloggers, Toby Bloomberg, provided some insights for businesses:

> Organizations are realizing that many of their customers are hanging out on blogs, in mash-up communities, on video sites, and on gaming sites. Just like in the traditional world of media, marketers want to have a presence where their customers are likely to be.
>
> Smart business people understand that new media offers multiple benefits, from enhanced search engine optimization, to new tools to obtain customer feedback and additional value-add content. Where social media really shines is creating relationships, which is the first step to customer acquisition and the reinforcement of customer retention.
>
> However, social media is more than a passive Web site strategy. The most beneficial aspect is the ability to engage directly with customers and other stakeholders. Social media opens the doors for businesses to listen to the unfiltered voices of their customers and to track those conversations. Social media also provides opportunities for the *people* within the company to join in on those conversations and talk directly to customers. Taking an active role in creating a dialogue with customers about issues that they care about, at the moment in time when they care about those concerns, is the heart of new media marketing.[21]

My personal experiences working with businesses that have experimented with new media as a way of engaging its target audiences have been astonishing:

- Bartleby Press, a book publisher, sold 1500 advance copies in one day using a targeted outreach strategy, bulletin boards, blogs, and MySpace.[22]

- FortiusOne, a Web mapping company, used social media to create excitement about its map images, in turn becoming a Web 2.0 sensation and a media darling, filling its sales pipeline…in one week.

- Reston Limo, a Washington, D.C. region transportation company, has garnered significant media attention and increased credibility through the CEO's blog.

- McGuire Associates, a very small accounting firm, has a constant, daily dialogue with customers via the CEO's blog.

- Goodwill of Greater Washington used a multi-faceted social media strategy to change its image from thrift to vintage, and increased store traffic and sales.

On and on, the stories continue. New media allows companies to create valuable content for important communities, beginning a dialogue with them and attracting loyal buyers. Created with a purpose—whether it's personal entertainment, the publication of an online journal, or corporate promotion—these content forms are sticky, generating and keeping audiences' interest. Social media creation has given everyone a voice, good or bad, and thus provided great freedom.

Social Media Success Story: Making It Better

By Kristina Bouweiri, CEO of Reston Limousine

Deciding to build a blog was a leap of faith. Yet it seemed like the natural next step for the company. Reston Limousine prides itself on cutting-edge marketing techniques, which in turn have made us the top limousine service provider in the Greater Washington region. So I started learning about blogs.

When *Time Magazine* dubbed "You" the 2006 person of the year, the decision became easy. The strategy behind Make It Better had several key components:

- Because Washington is a very congested traffic region, discussing commuting woes and efforts to better our roads was a natural choice.

- Create a tangential value proposition for readers of the blog and the company's mission, as well as provide superior transportation services, that is our goal. The title "Make It Better" is a commitment to creating better commuting experiences.

- Make It Better entries let readers know that Reston Limo understands the issues they face on a daily basis and can help improve those situations.

- Use the blog to position me as an expert to the local Washington media on transportation related issues.

Branding matched the corporate identity standards to ensure continuity and integration with all of our outreach efforts. Several categories of stories, including Transportation Issues, Telework, and Go Green, were created. We then populated the blog with several stories and launched in late February, 2007.

It's only been four months, but the results have been

outstanding. Make It Better has been cross linked by several local transportation and metro area blogs. Our Web site has benefited with additional increased traffic and better search engine optimization.

We've already been featured on television on Fox-5 News in a spot positioning me as an expert, as well as a write-up in the *Washington Post*, a video spot for the *Washington Business Journal*, and a write-up in a National Limousine Industry magazine. Local bloggers are asking me to guest blog. In short, I am quickly becoming the anticipated regional business expert on local transportation related issues.

Even more important are the intangibles. When I walk into local networking events with CEO's and elected officials, they refer to my blog and ask me about my experiences. New business meetings often begin with a discussion about the blog and how much clients like it. More than just a cute marketing development, the blog has become an integral tactic within our overarching communications program. It's safe to say that new media will continue to be part of our marketing repertoire as we continue to expand our business.

Corporate America's Challenge

As the social media revolution progresses and businesses enter the game, content will continue to evolve, and that means better quality and more interesting new media for all of us. And, of course, bad content will not survive very long, forcing businesses into a Darwinistic survival of the new media world's fittest. This is a natural course of life, not just for new media. And in this particular instance, great content is king.

That creates a big problem for corporate marketers and

PR practitioners who are used to playing by the rules of command and control, and having defined methods of engagement with the media.[23] Heretofore, they could issue whatever content they wanted and it was taken, because there were controlled forms of communication. Content is now out of control, being created by millions. And there's very little that traditional marketing and public relations professionals can do about it.

With each passing day, the gap between outdated tactics and current marketing needs widens. It's incumbent upon communicators to learn new media, not just on a theoretical level, but as practitioners. Without new media, our ability to effectively counsel executives and clients is incomplete. The revolution's impact on real business marketing campaigns demands our professional attention.

Practitioners are now faced with the inevitable. There is no pragmatic argument that can sway the facts. New media is here to stay. Marketers and PR practitioners know that their companies and clients should engage with their communities and dialogue with them on their terms via social networks.

At the same time, corporations are faced with the uncomfortable reality that they need to behave better. It's not okay to pull the wool over consumers' eyes anymore, because if they do put out a bad product, misrepresent the facts, or engage in unethical activity, the new media environment will surely attack the corporation's brand reputation. They will do so in an effort to warn other buyers and protect each other.

"Doc Searls talks about three mortalities, or what I like

to think of as business models, for Web 2.0 companies: self interest, accounting (scratch my back and I'll scratch yours) and generosity," said Kami Huyse, author of the popular public relations blog, "Communication Overtones."

"These can easily be applied to Social Media, such as blogging, podcasting and video-casting. I believe that the posture of generosity is essential to the Social Media culture."

Corporations must act with transparency, strong ethical behavior, an honest admission of wrongs, and prompt actions to correct wrongs. Further, they must use the same tools—new media forms—to communicate their positive actions. Now more than ever, companies must use new *and* traditional media to become part of their communities, and do so in an honest, relationship-driven way. Their brand reputations rely on it.

Recently, Marketing Daily's Karl Greenberg reported that Nissan has integrated its corporate citizenship and philanthropy program with its communications department. The resulting "haloization" of branding efforts is meant to build more trust in the corporate brand, building an image of citizenship that most companies haven't even conceived of.[24]

"In the past, corporate citizenship has been a series of random acts of kindness driven by interests of senior executives of a company, without a lot of research or a lot of strategy—a side activity," says Simon Sproule, Corporate Vice President/Global Communications, Corporate Social Responsibility and Investor Relations at Nissan. "If you look at an investment which is in the millions of dollars a year, trusting that to third parties is not the right way to manage our reputation and brand. When you are responding to someone else's program, it's never as good for you as if you went out and created it." [25]

This type of intelligent marketing and humanitarian effort is exactly what is needed to turn the tide against the increasingly negative image of corporate America. Rarely have philanthropic programs been this strategically engineered to enhance a communications effort.

To reach their constituents in new media environments, marketing communications and public relations professionals must steer their organizations correctly. Doing so will require a new approach to marketing, a different mindset and one that will not only dictate the way new media is used for business, but also new principles of communicating in general.

The rest of this book deals with the pragmatic basics of new media and integrating it within a larger marketing communications effort. It assumes that a company or a practitioner has at least a passing interest in social media, and that they have reached a point where there's a very real possibility of engaging in a social media strategy of some form.

Parting Thoughts

The online environment changed into a truly socially interactive world, where content users or readers have just as much impact as content makers. In this new era, social media networks like Wikipedia, Facebook, YouTube, and the advent of blogs are constantly evolving and changing the way people perceive communications. Users are more accepting of peer-generated and reviewed content than they are of traditional, company-developed articles or data.

The private sector must delve into this realm where

message control is lost, and value creation means more than any sales initiative. How can companies be successful in using social media? Even previously successful brands took months or years to achieve a social media victory. It takes an honest, community-centered effort to build a successful social media campaign.

The Migration to Social Media

An expansion of information choices has fueled the social media movement. Consumers, companies, and other members of the public can now communicate their opinions directly as opposed to relying on the media.

Blogs and other media offer more raw and authentic information, which readers increasingly prefer over what they perceive as the colder, more detached quality of traditional news sources. Companies that are targeting a new generation of buyers have noticed this preference shift, and have changed their outreach methods.

Impact on Businesses

When a business considers a social media campaign, its fears typically center on negative commenting. Allowing negative feedback to be shown on your own Web site goes against the traditional marketing culture of brand control.

Today's consumer, however, sees criticism and opposing voices as a measure of a company's openness to addressing its detractors rather than arbitrarily silencing them. Effective social media management can yield a much closer relationship with consumers, as well as valuable feedback back from them, be it positive or negative.

Corporate America's Challenge

Companies can no longer afford to rest on their laurels when it comes to engaging the media. New technologies are constantly evolving, and old techniques are simply not reaching as many consumers as they once did.

YouTube, Twitter, Facebook, and other user-generated content networks and mechanisms have created an environment where bad corporate behavior can no longer be hidden for very long and can quickly spiral out of control. A social media outlet allows for a direct connection with the consumer to build loyalty, create value, address concerns, and/or build goodwill.

Notes

[1] Adam Aleman, "Exposed: How Dem Part Operative Plan to Youtubing Republicans in 2008," FlashReport, May 22,2007 (http://www.flashreport.orgblog.php?postID =2007052203510081)

[2] Robb Tokatakiya, "The George Allen Implosion Continues," Tokatakiya, Otober 30, 2006 (http://tokatakiya.blogspot.com/ 2006/10/george-allen-implosion-continues.html).

[3] Don Tapscott and Anthony Williams, Wikinomics, Portfolio Publishing (New York, NY: 2006), p. 38.

[4] Susan Getgood, "More JetBlue Blues and some good advice from Strive," Marketing Roadmaps, March 4, 2007 (http:// getgood.typepad.com/getgood_strategic_marketi/2007/03/ more_JetBlue_bl.html)

[5] We recommend starting with David Meerman Scott's New Rules of Marketing & PR. For a full list of resources see the appendices.

[6] Doc Searl, "Syndication and the Live Web Economy," Linux Journal, December 9, 2005 (http://www.linuxjournal.com/article/8731).

[7] Original interview with Ike Pigott, June 25, 2007

[8] Shel Holtz, "Podcast: Interview with Ike Pigott "Hobson and Holtz report, June 2 (http://www.forimmediaterelease.biz/index.php/Weblogfir_interview_ike_pigott_american_red_cross_june_2_2007)

[9] Original interview with Ike Pigott.

[10] Ibid

[11] Kami Watson Huyse, "Interview: Red Cross Seeks Bloggers as Volunteers," Communciations Overtones, June 6, 2007. (http://overtonecomm.blogspot.com/2007/06/interview-red-cross-seeks-bloggers-as.html)

[12] Ibid

[13] Ike Piggot, "About this Site," American Red Cross Disaster News Portal, June 2, 2007 (http://redcross.wordpress.com/2007/06/01/about-this-site/)

[14] Ike Pigott, original interview.

[15] Seth Sutel, "Newspaper Circulation Falls 2.1 Percent," Associated Press, April 30, 2007.

[16] Pew Research Center, "Pew Research Center's report, "News Audiences Increasingly Politicized," June 8, 2004, p. 1(http://people-press.org/reports/display.php3?ReportID=215).

[17] "Web Attack," BusinessWeek, April 16, 2007, (http://www.businessweek.com/magazine/content/07_16/b4030068.htm).

[18] Wwekrazy, YouTube, February 23, 2007 (http://www.youtube.com/watch?v=su0U37w2tws).

[19] Frank Rose, "Commercial Break," Wired!, Vol 14, Issue 12, December 2006 (http://www.wired.com/wired/archive/14.12/tahoe.html?pg=1&topic=tahoe&topic_set=).

[20] Laura Ries, "Origin of Brands Author Laura Ries Discusses New Media," The Buzz Bin, April 23, 2007 (http://www.livingstonbuzz.com/blog/2007/04/23/origin-of-brands-author-laura-ries-discusses-new-media/).

[21] Toby Bloomberg, original interview, June 9, 2007.

[22] Disclosure: Bartleby Press published this book, too.

[23] Robert Scoble and Shel Israel, "Naked Conversations," (John Wiley & Sons: Hoboken, NJ, 2006) p. 100.

[24] Kami Watson Huyse, "Culture of Generosity in Social Media," Communications Overtones, April 19, 2006 (http://overtonecomm. blogspot.com/2006/04/culture-of-generosity-in-social-media.html).

[25] Karl Greenberg, "Nissan Moves to Create Corporate Citizenship Programs," MarketingDaily, April 16, 2007 (http://publications.mediapost.com/index.cfm?fuseaction=Articles.showArticleHomePage&art_aid=58725).

[26] Ibid.

Chapter 2
New Media Ready?

To be prepared for a new media strategy, first understand the rules of engagement. You must be prepared to give up control of the message, know the community you intend to participate in, commit resources, and embrace business transparency in full. This is not an easy thing to do, because users will suddenly want to be part of product development, understand how to use your service, and contribute to the overall experience of your product's target community. Your company must make a strategic decision whether or not to participate in this open environment.

Allowing millions of people to openly express their opinions, spark support, and expose weaknesses is intimidating to many businesses and is keeping them from participating. Truly, a brand manager or public relations professional is responsible for a company or a brand's reputation in all media forms. Companies risk brand reputation by not participating, but at the same time, they risk brand perception if they approach new media with a mindset of message and brand control without regard for two-way conversations. However, either way, as more and more companies embrace the new media era, competition will force companies to participate openly or lose market-share.

Authors Don Tapscott and Anthony Williams do a great job encapsulating this trend in their book Wikinomics. This $9 million research project turned into book goes into great detail about how online communities and group contribution benefits businesses. The result: "While some leaders fear the heaving growth of these massive online communities, Wikinomics proves this fear is folly. Smart firms can harness collective capability and genius to spur innovation, growth, and success."[1]

Blogger Joe Wikert encapsulated the Wikinomics principles, "*As they see it, the four keys to success are openness, peering, sharing and acting globally.*"[2] These principles, from a communications standpoint, are essential in the new media environment. As a marketing executive or a PR practitioner, it means that the principles of success in social networks demand openness, two-way conversation with community members, a willingness to share some valuable information, and a conscious effort to embrace your entire constituency. Basically, the key here is to start participating and conversing with the people that directly and indirectly affect your business. In new media, participation marketing, a concept created by Social Media Club

President, Chris Heurer.[3] And, if businesses would embrace this approach in all of their communications efforts, much less new media, the results would be amazing. Online communities are already realizing that benefit.

Social Media Success Story: Nuts About Southwest

One of the most well-known and liked corporate social media initiatives to date is the Southwest Airlines blog, Nuts About Southwest. This effort demonstrates strong principles in blogging including transparency, community building, and dialogue with customers about the message.

Southwest Airlines created the blog knowing that their message may be taken out of context, misunderstood, and diluted. Yet, because the brand—the customer experience—expresses itself beyond the blog through Southwest's consistent marketing, product, and employees, the company's message is not only propagated by blog readers, but also protected by them.

When interviewed on the topic of brand integrity, Southwest blog team member Paul Berg said, "There was a customer size issue that arose on the blogosphere (not on our site) that had become a really contentious issue for us. We felt it was necessary, since it was already being talked about on the blogosphere to discuss it on our blog. That was a perfect example of customers who didn't truly understand our policies and taking issues with them, but other customers came forward and corrected them, or clarified their misunderstanding about it."

Community Building

By dialoguing with their customers and the larger blogosphere, Southwest strengthened its brand and message by managing customer perception. Their approach does not control specific messages. Instead the Southwest

---

team responds to comments and tells their side of the story. When feedback about their service was strong enough or revealed weaknesses, they adapted to the situation.

For example, Southwest was getting complaints about people not being able to book their flights for the upcoming summer. Instead of trying to control the message, Southwest Schedule Planning Lead Planner, Bill Owen, wrote a blog entry telling the airline's side of the story. Blog readers were unhappy, hitting Southwest with 253 comments. As a result, Southwest expanded its scheduling window to 120 days. Owen explained these changes in several follow-up posts, including one called, "I Blogged, You Flamed, We Changed."

In another instance, Southwest was exploring alternate methods to their traditional open seating policy. The airline blogged their considerations. Lead Southwest blogger Brian Lusk explains the result:

The response we received from our existing customers was overwhelming, and their comments ran about 90 percent in favor of keeping open seating. Some of this came as correspondence, but we received about 700 comments to [Southwest Airlines CEO] Gary Kelly's two blog posts on this issue.

Although the issue has not been completely decided, we have made the decision that, if we stay with open seating, we never again will apologize for it and will consider it to be a proud Southwest difference. Additionally, some of those who favor open seating had concerns about our boarding process and submitted suggestions, which we carefully considered. The blog played a huge role because it concentrated those thoughts into one place.[3]

The Nuts About Southwest Blog has also become a personal communication medium. In one case, an employee's discussion of a medical condition caused a reader to explore a similar problem. That reader found out he had cancer, and as a result of the post, was able to treat it. The story unfolded live on the blog.

"The relationships we try to build with our customers have everything to do with [community], but also, yes, this unique business that we are in allows us to [be] part of people's lives," said Paula Berg. "We are with them for happy occasions, sad occasions, traveling to reunions and for all kinds of reasons. People will forever associate that with their experiences and the people on that flight who were kind to them or got them what they needed when they weren't feeling well, it is definitely a bonding-type of experience."

Resources

Southwest found that blogging was a major initiative from a resource perspective. As the blog became more popular, it took a life of its own. The comments and increased readership demanded that the team continue to evolve posts, the blog itself and add content creators.

"The sheer logistics of the blog, as it grows, is different," said Brian Lusk. "You have more comments to log, to make sure you have fresh posts. When the blog continues to grow you can't just put it out there and ignore it, it will die and people will lose interest. We went to a blog team asking for a few people to do 3 or 4 posts a month. The blog team only has to work a few hours over the course of a month which isn't a significant time investment."

In addition to 34 team bloggers, Southwest has two staffers working on the blog, plus back-up resources. There is a streamlined editing process to ensure quality posts. And then there's the technology; Southwest has its own server for the blog, which must be maintained independently of the company's IT systems.

An important aspect for Southwest was having senior leadership support the effort, post on occasion, and actively decide how to handle difficult comments. Everyone, including Southwest's CEO Gary Kelly, can be involved in various issues.

Lastly, the blog team ensures that posts match the company's ethical commitment with transparency into their operations. The result provides a public perception of the company that is an accurate representation of the work and family environment fostered at Southwest.

"The whole culture here is based around being honest, upfront, and the Golden Rule is one of our corporation's core values," said Brian Lusk. "We're not a religious company, but that rule kind of governs everything we do."

Diva Marketing Blog author, Toby Bloomberg, interviewed Simon Schneiders, CEO of BabyChums.com. This site is a classic example of the principle of Wikinomics at work. In the interview, Schneiders details how Babychums.com was an idea born without focusing on commercial drive but rather, what the market needs, the gap and embracing current technologies. The community is for the newly mothering female, ages 18 to 45, with little or no experience of social networking.

Babychum's is often the first entry for its users into networking via Free-Baby-Web pages. The site is simple, using classified advertising and other discreet promotions for revenue generation. The community works without a lot of help from the parent company, and drives content.

Representing one of the most powerful unions in all history, companies like BabyChums, and their community of customers, are contributing their thoughts, intelligence, insight, advice, feedback, opinions, etc. This content generation covers everything from reviews, blog posts, article comments, and creating their own sub-networks, to everything living online for others to see and build upon. It represents the true Wiki environment.

Perhaps the most interesting thing about user-generated content is the incredible influence members have on messaging. Their unchecked ability to comment at will via their blogs, via comments in wider social networks, enables them to dramatically reshape the way companies operate. Southwest airlines' decision to keep unassigned seating is a powerful example of how social networks can better a business and its relationship with important communities.

How does a company know if it's ready for new media? There are five steps that a business must embrace to know its social media initiative will work. They are:

1. Give up control of the message
2. Participate within your community
3. Is your community social media savvy?
4. Committing the resources
5. Understanding transparency and ethics

If you can check off these five benchmarks, then it is likely that the right new media strategy will be highly successful. (Chapter three deals with creating that strategy.)

Step 1: Giving Up Control of the Message

The first thing a marketer has to understand is that they cannot control the message within social networks. At best, marketers can influence, shape, and nurture them.

The ensuing dialogue from such efforts may provide some unexpected insights about your company.

For example, jetBlue was absolutely taken through the paces for its failure to cancel flights (and the ensuing inability to get their planes to the right destinations) during a Valentine's Day storm in 2007. Instead of using its blog to communicate with and about this issue (for example what the airline was doing to resolve its problems), the jetBlue corporate blog went silent, and traditional media relations were employed to communicate during the crisis. The blogosphere went crazy. A YouTube apology, issued weeks later, became scorned. The ensuing social network black eye still resided with jetBlue for months. Eventually jetBlue CEO David Neeleman resigned.

Here is a comment taken from a "60 Days Later, What Do You Think" posting from Shel Israel's popular Global Neighborhoods Blog[5]:

> I feel about the same about jetBlue—that they're a great, cheap way to fly to NYC. In fact, [a] week after next I'll be on one of their planes. However, if they leave us sitting on the tarmac for 3 hours, my perception will change completely and I will hate them utterly.
>
> So maybe this is how things have changed: before they might have had 2 or 3 chances to make mistakes before I disliked them as an airline. Now they have none.
>
> Posted by: *Maggie Fox* | *April 14, 2007 at 06:37 AM*

jetBlue's demonstration of how a company tried to control the message after engaging its constituency with a blog demonstrates that social networks cannot be easily controlled. This is a dramatic shift for communications professionals who have been trained to control the message. Prior to the new media revolution, the biggest danger to a company was a reporter that was feeling his or her oats. Or, if a consumer advocate started a grassroots PR campaign to highlight a wrong, attract attention and influence change. A not-so-everyday occurrence that only seemed to occur when scandals like Enron broke out, or a massive product recall occurred. Now every customer can say something.

It is only natural that you cannot contain social networks because they mirror human relationships. Assuming that social network behavior is equivalent to human behavior, we can analyze further. First, it is pretty much assumed that people in this country utterly detest being controlled. They resent it. However, people will listen, they'll even allow you to influence them and give your argument/product/service a chance—as long as you take their wants and needs into consideration. If your community finds that trust is broken for whatever reason (e.g. I'm not a crook, or nuclear weapons are a slam dunk), there's a whiplash effect that attacks credibility in very serious ways.

Returning to social networks, that means pros can't control new media forms like they used to. It's too egalitarian now. Consumers and communities are no longer beholden to monolithic traditional media forms, and can use new media to state their views...they don't have to submit to a managing editor for facts and they don't need to run corrections.

A paradigm shift of this nature requires a 180-degree shift in approach in how you tackle other marketing initiatives. If businesses intend to engage in social media outreach, they must resort to influence now. Controlling the message is a luxury of times past. Further, this influence is based on trust, so now more than ever, true relationship building is thrust upon corporate America. This means companies have to be honest, communicate, give as well as take, and be prepared for feedback.

It forces high ranking executives to jump back into customer relations—helping to foster dialogue between the people that make up the customer base and the executives running the company. It's creating a new level of customer service and accountability.

Giving up control is not a bad thing — in fact it's less about "giving up" and more about engaging. And to engage, you must first stop and think about why you should be part of the conversation. It injects a new step in the marketing process, which by default, makes the messaging process more transparent and genuine. Consider the valuable lessons that Southwest got from its community when they did not react well to the current scheduling policy and the possibility of assigned seating. Because the company listened to negative feedback, the airline was able to address its customers' wants and needs, and at the same time, made them feel engaged with the company. Lack of control worked to Southwest's benefit.

2. Participating in a Community

Like giving up control of the message, this step requires a sharp paradigm shift in the mind of the reader. For the past 80 years, mass media has allowed politicos, companies and organizations to broadcast their message to target audiences in a very controlled fashion. Masterminds have used these channels to market to their target audiences for both good and evil, from WWII politicos like FDR, Churchill and Goebbels, to modern masters Reagan, Clinton and Rove. Companies like Procter & Gamble, Nike and Microsoft have exploited markets throughout the world via controlled branding, PR and messaging.

Controlled messaging is the root of all "beauty" campaigns and it will remain such. But the difference between corporate brand promotion and community marketing is similar to broadcasting versus talking, listening, and reacting. New media destroys the idea of targeting your audience. Why? Because there is no more audience. The single notion that one message inspires everyone is absolutely ludicrous in the new world of community marketing.

Due to the rise of social networks in the past few years, the audience has become your community. A more Zen-like approach of attracting customers through community participation is preferred within social media.

No one better stated this than Jay Rosen in his *Press Think* article, "The People Formerly Known as the Audience:"

> You don't own the eyeballs. You don't own the press, which is now divided into pro and amateur zones. You don't control production on the new platform, which isn't one-way. There's

a new balance of power between you and us. The people formerly known as the audience are simply *the public* made realer, less fictional, more able, less predictable.[6]

Suddenly, the audience doesn't like being talked down to...in fact, they feel insulted by it. Mike Sansome in his ConverStations Blog succinctly stated, "Subliminally, there tends to be an Us vs. Them mentality when a barrier stands between you and your customer." [7]

So it is. And while that was effective in the years prior, it won't work in the new media environment. That's because mass communications as we know it is dead. It has been dead for some time. There are hundreds of television channels and radio stations, as well as a plethora of Web-based video services. There are millions of blogs out there. The citizen journalists of the world have already arisen. The often discussed revolution has already passed.

Even traditional mass advertising is changing, influenced by the new media around it. KFC has started campaigns with promotional codes embedded in each commercial to drive people to the KFC online community. During the Super Bowl, Doritos ran advertising segments generated by Doritos fans. Pizza Hut also pointed customers to a Web site where they could order their pizza for a discount during the Super Bowl.

Now—meaning the now of our target audience/mass communication trained minds—is gone. To be successful, a business has to change its thinking. Instead of standing on a speaker box and dictating propaganda to your audience, it is now time to take to the streets and interact with your community—one by one by one. Step two demands that a company look at marketing as an opportunity to engage its community—a privilege, not a right.

Some people feel the difference between an audience and a community is splitting hairs. However, there is an attitude difference. Similar to saying, you'll try to run a mile versus you will run a mile, targeting social media audiences versus participating in communities creates two different results.

A change of this nature is hard to take. Even writing this book, I kept writing target audiences, over and over. I was still stuck in my well-entrenched and trained approach towards PR and marketing. Contributing author Brian Solis quickly caught and urged me to eradicate the word audience throughout the text.

Communities have been the watch word of the new media revolution, but what does that really mean? It means we are returning to relationships. Everyone thinks it's a revolution, when in reality it's a return to old-fashioned values. Relationships and values in the sense of the baker, the butcher and general store owners down on Main Street. People want to know their vendors, they want to interact with them, and most importantly, they want to be heard! Instead, the small town feel is now a global phenomenon—creating millions of global micro-communities.

Historically speaking, this is not a new concept. Public trust is really about accountability—and that should apply whether it's business, government or charitable related activities. If you look up public trust on Dictionary.com, one result is "something (as property) held by one party (the trustee) for the benefit of another (the beneficiary)."[8] When a community trusts a business, they expect more than just a product, they expect their trust to be fulfilled over and over again. And marketing through social networks allows companies to dialogue and create the necessary trust invoked in the buying relationship. In fact, simply listening and participating strengthens this relationship.

If your company is ready to stand side-by-side with its customers online, there is great benefit from it. Feedback is less negative than one might think. Instead, it is more relational, a dialogue that allows the company to surpass challenges and develop better products and/or services for its community.

In a *Nation's Restaurant News* article, Diva Marketing Blog author Toby Bloomberg was cited as a subject matter expert. "You join the conversation," Bloomberg said. "It's a trite statement, but it's true. If someone says something about poor customer service, it is probably what others believe as well. Wouldn't it be better to address those issues on the blog?"[9]

No better example of this can be cited than the way Southwest turned more than 1,000 comments on two issues into new ways to validate their customers. Southwest understands that Nuts About Southwest is not a tactical propaganda mechanism, but a living, breathing conversation with its national community of travelers.

But if your company is not ready for this type of dialogue and community participation, it's best not to engage in new media promotion. One of the biggest sources of corporate failures in new media is treating the media form as a propaganda mechanism. It just doesn't work. Users get bored and stop visiting the blog or don't click through the ad, or stop the video. And they think less of you for it.

Step 3: Is Your Community Social Media Savvy?

There are many types of businesses out there, from fast food chains to defense contractors selling $300 million fighter jets. Each one has a community that buys its products, and gets information in its own particular way. Some are conservative, some are not. Age, gender, literacy, title, etc. all play into the demographics of a company's community, which is made up of several different role players: buyers, employees, investors, etc.

Before deciding whether or not to blog, it's worth looking at your community to determine if they will be receptive to such outreach. Does your community match the social networking profile?

The Pew Internet/American Life Project issued a report in July of 2006 detailing the profile of a blogger:

8% of Internet users, or about 12 million American adults, keep a blog. 39% of Internet users, or about 57 million American adults, read blogs—a significant increase since the fall of 2005.

The most distinguishing characteristic of bloggers is their youth. More than half (54%) of bloggers are under the age of 30. Like the Internet population in general, however, bloggers are evenly divided between men and women, and more than half live in the suburbs. Another third live in urban areas and a scant 13% live in rural regions.

Another distinguishing characteristic is that bloggers are less likely to be white than the general Internet population. 60% of bloggers are white, 11% are African American, 19% are English-speaking Latino and 10% identify as some other race. By contrast, 74% of Internet users are white, 9% are African American, 11% are English-speaking Latino and 6% identify as some other race.[10]

Much has occurred that has inspired widespread adoption of blogging, including the first major wave of businesses who are trying social network technology for marketing, customer relationship and sales purposes. New social networks like Facebook, Twitter, Squidoo and others are engaging communities en masse.

Nevertheless, the demographics speak for themselves. If your community is populated with folks over 50 and not in some sort of communications field (journalism, marketing or publishing), then it probably does not make sense to create a blog or engage in social networks, rather to monitor their behavior with traditional and new media. This is going to be the next big frontier for new media, and the foundation for reaching these groups of people is already well underway. It will be proven in the next Presidential election and every election thereafter. In fact, even in the primaries, Democratic candidates are tapping new media as a way of reaching people of all demographics and age groups. Consider the incredible social network strategies already deployed—MyMcCain, Obama's campaign supporter blog networks, and Hillary Clinton's YouTube efforts.

How do you know if new media will work for you? What is the right benchmark? When should you commit?

If even 15 to 25 percent of your buying community is doing it or if a significant portion of your revenues are attributed to the right demographic, then it's time to start and invest the necessary effort into new media strategies. Enough of your current constituency is up and running, and the business value of engaging your community in this type of conversational relationship is invaluable.

Consider it an ongoing focus group where your clients constantly dialogue with you, and they appreciate it! This important minority segment of your business will expand over time as adoption increases, and generations X and Y begin to dominate the workforce.

Step 4: Dedicating the Resources

The most well known form of social/new media is blogging. It's also the most mature, with the slowest amount of actual current growth, according to *BusinessWeek*.[11] By the time this book is published, individual consumer blogging will probably have already peaked at 100 million different blogs, according to Gartner Group.[12]

Peaked, in our opinion, is debatable. Blogs with text, video or a combination thereof will be an everyday form of business conversation. The primary driver of Gartner's predictions for the maturation of the adoption curve is that blogging requires commitment, not just of financial resources, but also of time and thought. This is not only true of blogging, but any social network activity, whether it's getting noticed in Digg or Stumble Upon or opening a storefront in Second Life.

In a Marketing Profs interview with Michael Stelzner,

Pete Blackshaw, CMO of Neilson BuzzMetrics, said, "I love my blog and its topic, but frankly, I'm struggling to keep up. I'm just not cranking out content like I used to, and feel as if I'm contributing 'too little, too late.' I'm starting to freak about folks potentially sending unsubscribe pings my way, and I just can't handle the thought of such rejection." Blackshaw explains, "Creating great and compelling online content takes real work and commitment."[13]

Failure to prepare for the necessary effort will more than likely result in a stalled effort. In Heather Green's *BusinessWeek* Blog entry about most users' reasons for stopping she writes:

> Excited to try out a new way of connecting with folks online, people flocked to blogging. But after an average of three months, most bloggers realize that blogging isn't for them. Since the community reading blogs continues to grow, this classic tech cycle of hype and maturity is good news for the remaining blogs. Those left standing are the influencers that attract members to their community and advertisers.[14]

And while Green is right about a greater opportunity for leadership, it also means that the potential for an abandoned effort is greater.

There are real resource issues for businesses:

Financial: If there is a physical presence to your new media effort, then don't go cheap with a free blogger template, minimal advertising or shabby storefront space. Spend some money and create a nice landing page, a blog template or a storefront that works within your larger branding effort. Integrate your campaign. Circuit City invested in IBM's capabilities to create a significant storefront within Second Life.[15]

Time: This is the big one. If you are a small business, you should prepare to have someone dedicated to your blog or other social network activity for at least eight to ten hours a week. Agencies serving their clients should ask for a minimum of 30 to 40 hour-a-month retainer. A larger company will need to commit more resources. If you use an agency, publicly disclose their involvement to avoid controversy.

Thought: Part of participating in a social network is investing the necessary time to create valuable information for the network. In essence, a business must have something to say. The next chapter deals with this topic in full, but from a resource perspective, this is not something to simply dump on the college intern. Senior leadership needs to be involved.

In some ways, it would be better not to start at all than to be seen online with a big social media effort that simply disappears or stops with a static blog or a non-participating avatar. Most mature new media users have seen these failed starts, and are skeptical of newer entities online. As a result, there is a wait and see period for newer players. A business must really commit to new media if it wants to succeed in this realm.

Something to consider here is that while paving the way for all forms of new media, the initial sets of pioneers should start grooming apprentices because as the conversation broadens, the time and passion commitment will only grow. In the first era of Web marketing, we saw the rise of the CMO (Chief Marketing Officer). There will be a need to build a team dedicated to fostering online communities and conversations within them. A new kind of CMO will emerge, Community Management Officer— or simply a community management team.

Step 5: Ethics and Transparency

This is a touchy requirement, but it is a critical one, too. A company must be what it represents itself to be, or it risks great peril with the new media portion of its de-mographic community.

At Livingston Communications and FutureWorks, we tell clients that a brand is a commitment, a promise to your community. It is also a living and breathing entity that, now more than ever, is co-created by the people. This brand is represented three ways; the first two are visually (ads, creative, Web site, etc.) and verbally (written word, Web site, oral communications, etc.). The third way is the most important—the experience. If the experience does not match the promotion via words and visuals, then the community feels betrayed and the brand develops a bad reputation. Once a brand is of ill-repute, it is very hard to recover that trust.

In the new media world, there is little tolerance for companies that aren't authentic in their representation. The experience must match the content creation online. Internet users already suspect big business and corporate America, and as such, new media initiatives are often on

a shorter leash. That's because most people are not interested in being part of a community that tolerates or enables unethical behavior. Most online communities expect
some level of transparency into corporate members' activities. This type of trust demands that corporate entities behave in the community's interest. There is a level
of tolerance for human errors, but a company must be
transparent and act ethically, communicating how it is re-
solving its errors to the benefit of all.

If a company does not communicate transparently
during times of crisis (a la jetBlue), then it will not be
well regarded by its online community. Its blog will lose
stature, its efforts within social networks will receive negative comments, and eventually (or immediately, depending
on the situation) its brand reputation will erode. In short,
if your company has not traditionally been open in its
dialogue with customers, this should be a red flag for you.
The company may not be new media ready.

Further, if the company has a penchant for ending up
in questionable ethical situations or its work is top secret,
then new media is likely to be a place to hear complaints.
While it may be a good idea to restore public trust, there
will be little current marketing value from such an effort.
Here are some examples of behavior that may cause distrust:

- Halliburton's contracting practices within the
  federal government
- ENRON's financial crisis
- O.J. Simpson
- National Security Administration (anything)

The point is that trust needs to occur in social networks of any kind. Without trust, there is little hope of success. It's better to invest the time and effort towards becoming a better corporation that can address and resolve these issues.

Parting Thoughts

Is your business prepared for a social media program? Can you commit to loss of message control, consumer correspondence, knowledge of community, substantial resource obligations, and business transparency? These necessary things create the foundation of valuable social media platform.

Successful social media campaigns are built on a foundation of feedback and communication. When a company communicates with people who directly or indirectly affect their business, they are able to build a better relationship with their constituency. Content is the push within a social media campaign, but the community is what keeps it going and allows it to accelerate.

Giving up Control of the Message

Corporate control of the message does not exist in the new media environment. Social media network users often comment about a company's perceived flaws despite traditional media coverage. By taking consumers' concerns into account, corporations can relay their message directly and address feedback accordingly. This minimizes consumer frustration or anger, and simply lets the user be heard. By responding to customer comments publicly through social media, a company is held in higher regard.

Participating in a Community

This new media "revolution" returns business to older values. Two centuries ago it wasn't just about business. It was about neighbors or friends who helped each other. Social media has made that possible again, albeit on a much larger scale, with a plethora of micro-communities that interact with each other. By talking with its communities, rather than at them, a company becomes an integral part of those communities.

Is Your Community Social Networking Savvy?

With 54 percent of bloggers under the age of 30, organizations that appeal to a largely older crowd, would not be well served in creating a blog or social networking campaign. However, even if 15 to 25 percent of a company's buyers are in that range, then it is wise to address these customers in the social media space. The social media dialogue can be thought of as a continuous focus group. New forms become more valuable as time progresses and users of social networks mature and enter the workforce.

Dedicating the Resources

The Internet's littered with failed corporate blogs and discontinued social media initiatives. Many simply can't think of new, interesting content to post, and with the time necessary to commit to a blog, many simply decide to stop. Content creators must diligently engage the community with appealing content for the life of the new media initiative, not just for the first few months. Having a unique look helps catch the reader's eye. Keeping them there requires a constant creation of appealing content that only comes with a significant time and thought commitment.

Ethics and Transparency

A brand is a promise to your community. If the public's trust is broken by a company misrepresenting themselves with that promise, regaining trust will be difficult. Community members expect transparency in a corporate social media effort, especially in crisis situations. Further, they expect a company will knowingly represent itself in an ethical fashion.

Notes

[1] Don Tapscott and Anthony Williams, Wikinomics Web site (www.wikinomics.com/book/index.php).

[2] Joe Wikert, "Wikinomics," Publishing Blog 2020, January 6, 2007 (http://jwikert.typepad.com/the_average_joe/2007/01/wikinomics_by_d.html).

[3] Chris Heurer, "Participation is Marketing, The Future of Communities," March 12, 2007 (http://www.futureofcommunities.com/2007/03/12/participation-is-marketing/).

[4] Brian Lusk, "Nuts About Southwest Demonstrates True Social Interaction," The Buzz Bin, May 8 (http://www.livingstonbuzz.com/blog/2007/05/08/nuts-about-southwest-demonstrates-true-social-interaction/).

[5] Toby Bloomberg, "Building Community with Online Communities-Part Two," Diva Marketing Blog, April 12, 2007 (http://bloombergmarketing.blogs.com/bloomberg_marketing/2007/04/building_commun.html).

[6] Shel Israel, "Jet Blue: How Do You Feel About Them Now," Global Neighborhoods April 13, 2007 (http://redcouch.typepad.com/ Weblog/2007/04jet_blue_how_do.html)

[7] Jay Rosen "The People Formerly Known as the Audience," Press Think, June 27, 2006 (http://journalism.nyu.edu/pubzone/ Weblogs/pressthink/2006/06/27/ppl_frmr.html).

[8] Mike Sansome, "Get Out from Behind the Counter," ConverStations, April 24, 2007 (http://www.converstations.com/ 2007/04/get_out_from_be.html)

[9] The Free Dictionary, "Publi + Trust" (http:// www.thefreedictionary.com/public+trust).

[10] Liza Berger, "Restaurants wade into social media to hook 'virtual' customers, "National Restaurant News, April 26, 2007 (http:// www.nrn.com/article.aspx?id=339090).

[11] Amanda Lenhart and Susan Fox, "Bloggers: A portrait of the Internet's new story tellers," Pew Internet & American Life Project, July 19, 2006 (http://www.pewinternet.org/pdfs/ PIP%20Bloggers%20Report%20July%2019%202006.pdf)

[12] Heather Green, Blogspotting, BusinessWeek.com, April 27, 2007 (http://www.businessweek.com/the_thread/blogspotting/archives/ 2007/04/blogging_growth.html).

[13] GartnerGroup, "Gartner Highlights Key Predictions for IT Organizations and Beyond" December 13, 2006 (http:// www.gartner.com/it/page.jsp?id=499323).

[14] Michael A. Stelzner, The Dark Side of Blogging: Warnings From Leading Bloggers, The Marketing Profs (http:// www.marketingprofs.com/7/dark-side-blogging-warning-leading-bloggers-stelzner.asp)

[15] Green, BusinessWeek.

[16] Ryan Olson, Circuit City Goes Virtual, Red Herring, December 15, 2006 (http://www.redherring.com/ Article.aspx?a=20280&hed=Circuit+City+Goes+Virtual& sector=Industries&subsector=InternetAndServices).

Chapter 3
Building a New Media Effort

Your organization is ready for its new media effort. Great! Now what? Well, more often than not it's time to figure out what kind of new media effort your company will engage upon. Many organizations opt for a blog, but this may not be the best use of your resources. For example, Coca-Cola decided to enable residents of Second Life, an open-ended virtual world, to create their own cyber-Coke machine instead of a blog.

Typically when engaging in a marketing effort, companies map out their product strategy, and the audiences that they want to market towards. The more successful ones research their audience before they engage, understanding their buyers' needs. Marketers often set up communications tactics to reach their targets and compel them to act. Measurements are created to determine the success of these efforts. Then, a campaign is launched.

Remember, audience-based approaches can negatively impact a company in the new media realm, therefore a community approach should be used. With a change of attitude and tone, most of the same principles apply; namely research and selection of new media vehicles based on the likelihood of success and resources.

Successful marketing campaigns have good marketing, but superior marketing usually only works when there's something valuable to offer. Truly exceptional marketing campaigns make strong products and services sell quicker, and bad products fail faster.[1] This paradigm applies to the new media world, too, only at warp speed. So be sure that your product/service/idea is ready for prime time *before* engaging in a new media initiative.

These four steps can help you determine what to communicate and how:

1. Focus on the community's interests
2. The Editorial Mission: Build value for the community
3. Who and what
4. Inspire your community to believe

Focus on the Community's Interests

A community's interests lie at the heart of any new media initiative, from business discussions to the newest Hollywood gossip. Initiatives succeed when companies and organizations create content that serves its communities' interests.[2] Remember, it's about the members of the social network.

Understand who your community really is. If you have a community of 50 rocket scientists in the western United States, create your initiative for them, not the entire blogosphere. Whether they are affiliated en masse with a community like Facebook or simply are philatelists who use blogs to discuss their latest stamp finds, a community enjoys specific types of information and content that is relevant to them.

"Forget the Technorati 100 thinking," said *Like It Matters* author, Brian Oberkirch, in a Buzz Bin interview. "Being famous to 15 people is a huge advantage if they are the right 15 people. Keep in mind that blogging mostly has indirect effects: You are building an online resume for yourself that is going to reward you in ways you really can't predict. Honor your readers' time. Give them great stuff to think about."[3]

Information types and discussions rarely include organization-based propaganda unless the public discussion revolves around a specific cause. In those cases, organization-based initiatives are often discussed, with merits and defects bantered about. This does not mean a company should outright pitch to the public, as this might be found offensive, particularly from an unknown player within the network. Not only do communities have unique information needs, they also have unique forms of engagement. Even if the company is a well recognized brand, it still makes more sense to research the community before taking any outbound activity.

Research remains the primary form of intelligence gathering for your potential social network. There are several ways to understand which social media forms and voices are the most important to your company's effort. First, begin with searching social media and blog directories (Technorati, Google, Ice Rocket and BlogCatalog.com) using keywords. Explore these blogs, video sites, social networks and Web portals thoroughly.

Second, determine which new media creators are leading your industry. Technorati's authority system is flawed, but does provide a rough benchmark of which social media outlets get the most attention. This system links to a blog or portal to determine the authority of the outlet. Authority does not necessarily mean that the blog is well respected, as the links may be negative or bolstered by paid-for reviews and/or link-baiting, and links do not equate to traffic or RSS subscriptions. Nor does Technorati's authority effectively measure the most important users in social networks, like YouTube or MySpace.[4] Still, at the time of writing, Technorati's authority rankings offer the best system out there for initial blog research.

Once preliminary community leaders are identified, get to know their content. Dive deep, read the information, consume the content they link to in their posts or honor rolls, and notice how the community interacts with these thought leaders. Learn what content excites the community by measuring the most popular posts and media, this can be judged by comments, referrals and link-backs. Study how topics make it to the forefront.

Your organization may even want to begin participat-

ing by commenting and adding general content to the
mix, but be careful about discussing corporate information until your organization fully comprehends its new
media strategy. Further, understand that your voice may
not be respected until the company makes significant con-
tributions to the community.[5] Corporate messaging will
not work effectively in the social media world. Instead,
try to just be a part of, and start building some early
goodwill and relationships. Also learning how to participate as a community member will help establish positive
relationships.

"The best thing a business can do is cultivate an understanding [of] the culture," said Toby Bloomberg, author of the Diva Marketing Blog. "Blogging/social media is
unlike any other marketing strategy I've seen. It is built
on a culture that incorporates community, and as with
any community, there are social norms that newcomers
must know about. Informal checks and balances are in
place and if you color outside of the lines, the blogosphere
is not shy about letting you know.

"Frequently that slap on the hand is not contained
within the confines of a few blog posts, but instead is
picked up by mainstream media. The impact to the goodwill of the brand or business may be significant. The most
critical aspects to keep top of mind are honesty, transparency, [and] authenticity."[6]

It is important to explore competing initiatives from
other companies and organizations. Check if they're respected by the community, if they're being discussed and
how (negatively or positively). See how the community

reacts to corporations and entities selling to them, and how other companies have successfully turned the community into advocates for their services. Analyze their efforts in comparison to your research findings about what makes the community tick. Some of these efforts will have failed and it is important to note why.

You can use formal market research studies conducted via surveys of social network members. Networks like Facebook and LinkedIn, offer these direct access forms of research.[7] Of course, many members will not take the survey, mirroring similar survey results in the brick and mortar world, too.

Your findings create an understanding of community interests, observations, and interactions that can direct a successful new media effort. Most importantly, a gauge of what's valuable to the community should be obvious. The roadmap to creating successful content should be available to you. There should be strategic pointers, including specific subject areas, types of popular stories and content. Use these trends to create the basis of an editorial mission for the new media effort.

The Editorial Mission: Build Value for the Community

It may seem parochial in nature, but one thing new media creators can learn from traditional media outlets is the creation of phenomenal content targeted towards a particular community. Garnering thousands or even millions of readers (depending on the size of the community) requires superior content, continued innovation and ongoing creativity.

"In order to implement a successful strategy, think like a publisher," said David Meerman Scott in his new book, *The New Rules of Marketing & PR*. "Marketers at the organizations successfully using the new rules recognize the fact that they are not purveyors of information, and that they manage content as a valuable asset with the same care that a publishing company does."[8]

Great publications use an editorial mission to guide their content creation to fulfill a purpose. The content is written to educate or inform readers, listeners or viewers about a particular or general subject matter. If content wavers from the mission, it's often discarded by a managing or executive editor whose job revolves around fulfilling the editorial mission and serving the community.

"Our [editorial mission's] focus is really on the reader, and I think that is more true now then ever before," said Chris Dorobek, Editor-In-Chief of *Federal Computer Week* and author of *The FCW Insider Blog*. When asked if an editorial mission could apply to a blog, Chris replied, "The short answer: Absolutely. As I mentioned, we are there to help people get their jobs done more effectively. But a part of that involves building a community, and I think blogs can play a key role in that."[9]

Unfortunately, a classic public relations error involves not understanding targeted publications' missions and what they write about. This often leads to horrific rants from reporters, some of which make it to the blogosphere (for examples, see the bad pitch blog).[10]

Marketing minds have to understand the importance of editorial missions, not only for outbound PR efforts, but for their own new media efforts. By sticking to an editorial mission statement, the new media content stays on track, creating value for its community by providing regular, intelligent copy, pictures, audio and/or video, that stays on topic.

Creating value builds opportunity in a win-win fashion for both your organization and your larger community. In this particular instance, valuable and well structured content towards a particular social network's needs allows you to contribute, participate and garner respect. By creating content that better suits the social network's needs, they will inherently come to trust your effort, and will want to work with you.

"How cool would it be for [BMW loyalists] to interface directly with a BMW representative on a regular basis," asked Todd Defren of SHIFT Media. "Pretty cool. And more importantly, it would present customers and prospective buyers with a highly-trafficked blog that BMW truly cared about. I recognize that there are challenges for any company to scale, including training and monitoring a group of "community managers" that could serve as adjuncts to the marketing group. But [what] is worth doing that *isn't* going to be a challenge?"[11]

And that's really the rub. Going through the difficulty of creating value for the community so they find it worthwhile (a.k.a cool for BMW owners). This requires a) knowing what the community wants, b) understanding the intrinsic value the company has to offer, and c) being creative enough to deliver this value in a way that's interesting and compelling. This is where the art of marketing can help your new media initiative.

There's one major pitfall to avoid in an editorial mission: Trying to overtly promote the company. This error remains one of the most common reasons corporate new media initiatives fail. Companies engage in social media because they want to market themselves, and they think new media forms are just another way to promote their wares. This error creates blogs that are never read, videos that are never played, and podcasts that buyers don't download.

There's no better example of this than the Wal-Mart corporate blogging scandal. This fake blogging or "astroturfing" incident demonstrated that Wal-Mart was more interested in tricking readers into believing the company was genuine in its correspondence. Instead, most citizens found Wal-Mart to be a profiteering, dishonest company, which permanently hurt the company's image. In an informal poll, Copywrite's Rich Becker found more of his readers saw Wal-Mart's flog as the biggest social media ethics transgression to date (36 percent).[12]

Promotional blogs bore the casual social network member. Sales pitches have no inherent value to someone who's interested in the company's general category. Getting "sold to" by corporations fails to meet the casual users needs and defeats the reason behind their use of the social media form in question. Content must appeal to the community, and this means delivering valuable, interesting new media initiatives. Promotion only works when it creates substantial value for your community. That doesn't mean a corporation should create yet another "day in the life" blog.

"If you want to create a blog that covers your industry rather than offering the typical company diary, that's fine too—even if the blog Pharisees criticize you for not adhering to blog orthodoxy," said Scott Baradell, President of IdeaGrove. "Ultimately, it will be the quality of what you produce that will matter—not whether your ideas fit into someone else's box."[13]

Content should be authentic, providing information that's inside the organization's natural and obvious areas of expertise. The organization's knowledge is its primary source of value to a community. Sharing relevant and interesting subject matter-specific content allows the company to build its image as a community leader or expert.

Business is complex, and in many ways, a simple subject matter may not be enough. Content can span several categories to create enough flexibility for the organization to discuss several initiatives. For example, GM's Fastlane has specific content areas, namely: Auto Shows, Bob Lutz, Business, Cars & Trucks, Design, Podcasts and Photo Albums.[14]

GM's Fastlane captivates audiences because it talks about developments within their product line (as opposed to the latest finance deal), new engines, race track initiatives and more. When they write about the business, it's a debate and a conversation. For example, a June 1, 2007 post featured a discussion started by the *USA Today's* negative view of GM's brands.[15]

Social Media Success Story: Getting in the FastLane

Foreign, and for the most part Japanese, automakers, have dominated American car sales, with the traditional

"Big 3" domestic manufacturers unable to respond. Increasingly, American buyers doubted the ability of the big three to counter foreign auto makers progress, and the blogosphere reflected this consumer attitude.

Bob Lutz, General Motors' 73-year-old vice-chairman, wrote a detailed response to blog posts he had read criticizing the Saturn brand on a return flight from Europe. Lutz wanted to publish his opinion, and GM's VP of Communications, Gary Grates, promptly exported the text to a moveable type template. This online post became the start of GM FastLane.[16]

GM had weighed blogging for some time, and experimented with the Small Block Engine Blog to commemorate the 50th anniversary of the engine. Lutz's piece however, pushed the company a step further. Important bloggers, like Neville Hobson, heralded the FastLane Blog as a milestone because it represented the first time a senior manager of a non-tech, Fortune 500 Company was a primary contributor to a blog. In addition, the almost instantly achieved quality of high readership and large amount of feedback proved that a largely recognizable brand's blog can thrive.[17]

FastLane had three distinct communities it served: car enthusiasts interested in developments at GM, normal, everyday customers, and investors, who want to know business and market information about the company. Each of these communities read FastLane and had individual bloggers posting on their own sites. FastLane served all of these parties with posts covering auto shows, Bob Lutz, business, cars and trucks, design, and LeMans. Additional social media includes podcasts and photo albums.[34] Video blog entries are now posted from car shows and racing events. GM also runs multiple blogs on a variety of topics, inside and outside of the company.

GM has had to deal with tough issues since the blog

has been running. In late 2005, it was revealed that they planned to fire close to 30,000 hourly workers in lieu of budget constraints, and in late-spring 2007, they were ridiculed for their opposition to a senate mandate of higher fuel economy in all U.S. cars. The blog though, has helped GM mange the backlash and communicate their point of view to their readers and the public at large.

Posts on FastLane are regularly attracting upwards of 20 comments as the popularity of the blog continues to grow. While there are plenty of argumentative comments posted by readers, there are even more positive ones. This open line of communication, where no one, regardless of views, are ignored, has helped GM's financial reemergence.[34]

On March 7th 2007, Rasmussen Reports issued poll results showing GM being viewed favorably by 69% of Americans, 21% higher than the same figure taken the previous July. This compared to the other Big 3 automakers, Ford and Chrysler, who posted 57% and 51% favorability ratings respectively. [4567]

With an editorial mission that provides content for your community that's relevant to the organization's day-to-day activities, a new media content strategy is born. And though the editorial mission may change over time as the new media initiative evolves, the mission guides content creation ensuring that it stays on track.

Also important are editorial standards that give general guidance for content creation. For example, encouraging cross-linking and references to other blogs, or avoiding attacks on others, etc. Videos should be limited to three minutes. These standards help your effort become consistent, and known to its community. While guidelines should be flexible, without them your content can wander.

Who and What

It's important to assign voices to the new media effort. Who's the content director? In some cases, the voice is that of the CEO, and in others, it's a social media director. Increasingly, because of the incredible amount of resources required, it's a team effort. Knowing who's going to create content, and when, is essential for success. Further, communicating who the authors are to the community is equally important. Titles matter, but not that much. In many cases, an actual line manager can have as much credibility, if not more, than a top ranked executive.

Debbie Weil writes in her blog, BlogWrite, for CEOs, "GM's FastLane Blog is managed by a team that includes Christopher Barger, GM's Director of Global Communications Technology (love the title), along with Alicia Dorset, who is titled 'Blog Editor.' I know that GM also works closely with their PR/interactive agency, Haas MS & L on the blog."

There's great debate about the authenticity of the voice. There's no shame in creating a team, someone who's assigned to blogging or creating podcasts. At the same time, having a CEO dictate news to a blogger or staff member who then creates the post for him enters a gray area. The reality is that CEOs don't have time to write great amounts of blog posts, but having them participate as part of the content creation team makes the effort better.

The debate about disclosure is a touchy one. Because of the rise of blogs, and their roots in inherent transparency, many people on the Internet feel that full transparency of content creators should be disclosed. Others feel that business blogging is a natural evolution, and with that evolution comes a change in the unwritten rules. We recommend transparency.

"If a business leader ultimately does opt to have someone else handle the writing of the blog, he should disclose it," said well-known marketing guru Shel Holtz. "What's the harm in a statement like this on an executive blog: 'Welcome to my blog. Several times each week, I articulate my thoughts to Mary Jones, who runs communications for the company, and she posts them here ensuring that I make the points I want to make. But rest assured, while Mary makes me sound better, the messages you read are mine; they come from my heart and I read all the comments myself.'"[18]

"Here's what a blog is: A series of entries on a Web site that appear in reverse chronological order, per the standards of blogging software," said Scott Baradell in a poignant Media Orchard entry. "Beyond that, have at it! Do what you want with the format! Change it. Expand it. Adapt it to your specific needs...if it's of value, people will read it. If it's a bunch of PR fluff, they won't—no matter who composes the words. CEOs don't have the time (or in many cases the writing skills) to prepare their own speeches, letters to shareholders, and on and on. The same deal goes for blogs."[19]

Similarly, podcasts, maps and videos can be created or

authored by anyone. In these instances, featuring the voice or shooting the person that's attributed with authorship virtually ends the ghostwriting issue; however, many execs will have their teams write the content. Failure to disclose creates cries of fake blogging and "astroturfing" across the blogosphere. This can really damage your corporate brand.

We believe offering a disclosure statement that there are teams behind the blog writers makes sense. Almost every major corporate blog has disclosed in some way (via interviews or disclosure statements) that they have a team supporting the effort behind the scenes.

Once you know who will create content, create a publishing schedule to ensure regular entries. If content is to be created by the organization, this should be a responsibility tied to job performance. Otherwise, content tends to fall to the wayside in favor of more important day to day tasks.

Similarly, it's important to know what the team is trying to accomplish, and that means creating measurement goals for the content. Knowing how many readers you want, how many views you need, what image you hope to convey, and which products need to see an uptick in sales, are critical to determining the success of the project. Ultimately, while creating value for a community remains the primary strategic thrust of new media creation, an organization must be able to measure its worth.

There are many ways an organization can measure its worth, ranging from Google analytics and RSS subscription management services, to increased brand awareness measurements from groups like Forrester research, or measuring sales increases. Whatever the case may be, an organization should not be intimidated by the newness of the media forms. Results can and must be measured.

"While blogging's value can't be measured precisely, marketers will find that calculating the return on investment is easier than it looks," said Forrester Research's, Charlene Li, "...marketers can create a concrete picture of the key benefits, costs, and risks that blogging presents, and understand how they are likely to impact business goals."[20]

Inspire Your Community to Believe

By now, you know what the community wants, you have an editorial mission, you understand how to communicate to the audience, who's going to do it, and what you want to achieve. Now it's time to get out there and do it. That means creating great content delivered over a strong platform.

The dissemination platform, whether it is a blog or a more complicated social network, should be an important consideration. Invest the time, research the latest tagging, RSS, blogging and social media forms, as this is a serious initiative for your organization. There are many resources to research for best practices in this realm and we encourage you to explore them.[21]

In addition, bring professional resources to help create the initiative. Going cheap with a basic blogger template or a simple YouTube profile is not a great way to impress the community. It's important to create a professional appearance representative of your brand that lets the community know you are serious about the initiative.

Function and aesthetics need to combine here. At the same time, realize that the media form will likely evolve in a year or so and will need to be upgraded. Again, there are many resources for you to explore.

"Design does matter," said renowned blogger Darren Rowse. "I think it is one strategy that can really lift a blog to the next level and help create a great first impression for a blog—especially in its early days."[22]

The same principles apply to any media form. Simple elegance in a site design, whether it be to host podcasts or to share videos, can help your effort rise above many other community contributors. But great design alone cannot work without great content. In new media, content is truly king. Nothing can replace superior content that appeals to the community. It will attract attention and support from other content producers and readers.

In a published "Beth's Blog" discussion, Kevin Gamble revealed some of the reasons why his HighTouch effort has been so successful: "Our mantra has been (and will continue to be) that each page of content needs to stand alone. We also keep hammering that content needs to be content—not solely navigation—just related links that are directly related to the content."[23]

Consider the phenomena of Hillary Clinton's theme song campaign. A simple, well-designed video blog or "vlog" was created on YouTube, and was integrated into her main Web site and MySpace campaign. In some ways this was simpler but really no different in strategy than the rest of the early presidential campaigns. Her content was politically oriented and did not differentiate her from the competition.

Then came the campaign song initiative, a series of fun videos showing a humorous Hillary Clinton asking her fans to choose her 2008 theme song. This series of YouTube videos caused an incredible amount of publicity and excitement as well as general interest from YouTube viewers.[24] The campy "Pick My Campaign Song" campaign generated more than one million views and intelligently drew potential voters to the official Hillary site. Even better, it personalized a candidate that's often criticized for a cool demeanor.[25]

"Hillary Rodham Clinton wants YouTube viewers to pick her campaign theme song—and the response...has been music to her ears," said a related Associated Press article. "In both videos, Clinton sports a self-effacing attitude. She mocked her vocal abilities in the first post. The second features clips of people saying 'this is ridiculous' and 'are you freaking kidding me?' in response to the contest, along with Clinton making fun of some of the videos submitted."[26]

All in all, the Hillary YouTube effort demonstrated what great content can do in the right setting. Ultimately, regardless of what new media form it is, whatever the actual cause or topic may be, great content works in the right settings. Take the time to invest in creating great content that meets your editorial mission.

"There are no shortcuts to creating great content for your Web site," said Jake Mathews in a 10e20 blog post. "The best content takes time to generate and is created the old fashion way with strong, factual research, drafting methods, revisions, and great presentation/layout for the Web. You must be an expert in your subject matter, have research sources at your fingertips and creative efforts to back you."[27]

Lastly, getting the community to believe means you must create content regularly and in a manner that your users come to expect. That means adhering to a schedule of posts, videos or podcasts (or photos or maps) and constantly preparing yourself for new entries. When vacations occur, content should be created in advance.

"Regular [content creation] yields increased traffic as people begin to realize that your Web site is a current source of information and if there's a significant period of downtime, people will begin to unsubscribe from the feed," said Teli Adlam on her blog, OptiNiche. "Developing a blogging schedule will vary based on your needs, your current schedule, and your ability to prioritize. And if you're looking to become a professional blogger or turn your blog into a powerhouse, then you'll probably need to work on it."[28]

Readers, viewers and listeners all lose interest if a new or old community member becomes irregular—or worse, infrequent—with their content. New media creation requires consistency as well as relevant, interesting content. In fact, many social media users will take a wait and see approach to new entrants in the community, just to see if they are legitimate.

The BobMeetsWorld Blog author says the number one reason he unsubscribes from blogs is their failure to publish regularly. "If I don't see any updates in 3 to 4 days I assume you must have stopped blogging and went on to do something useful with your life," said Bob. "No reason for me to stick around anymore. I'm gone. Your spot is taken by someone's feed that *does* provide me with new stuff."[29]

Failing to follow up on your commitment to the community—a commitment to participate and provide value—demonstrates failure. Such black eyes are hard to recover from. It's better not to start at all than to end—or worse—slowly fade without warning. It will take three times the effort to rebuild a second new media effort that's successful, and the community will be wary of these repeated efforts.

Parting Thoughts

A company must determine what social media approach will yield the best results for them. Most companies choose a blog, but this is not always the correct choice. Assuming the community values the company's offering, then that company must research providing additional value through its campaign.

Successful social media campaigns focus on the community's interests while building value for the community via content and participation. It needs to be clear who is writing and what is trying to be accomplished, and that you are working to inspire the community to believe in the company and product.

Focus on the Community's Interests

An individual company must focus on what people it wants to influence. The target groups may be large, or they could be small. However, people outside of these groups should be of no concern to the company.

Page rank or Technorati authority may not be something that a company should be concerned about.

Through online research, a company must find where community members get information and how they like to be engaged. By knowing what the larger community likes, an organization is more likely to create social media that is of real value.

The Editorial Mission:
Build Value for the Community

Ensure that content has value for the readers. An editorial mission guides content creation. By tailoring content in a creative way and understanding what value the company itself has to offer, a company will garner respect from its core readership instead of turning them off with traditional PR, marketing, or "day in the life" entries. Multiple categories of entries or subjects are often necessary in order to keep the subject matter somewhat fresh. While there may be categorical diversity, it is important to stay relatively on track.

Who and What

Knowing who is responsible for creating content is vital for success. This doesn't have to be the highest ranked individual in the company, but readers enjoy both an authenticity of voice and true authoritative information from the organization.

Companies should reveal who the main content creators are. The authors should view the effort as a core responsibility while working towards tangible goals, such as views or number of readers, to truly measure and work toward its effectiveness.

Inspire Your Community to Believe

There is a two-prong approach to drawing in and keeping readers, which involves creating new, interesting content, and creating it on a consistent basis. This requires diligence. One must be a constant lookout for unique or new media that can be used to add something extra to the social media initiative.

Notes

[1] David Ogilvy, Ogilvy on Advertising (Vintage Books. New York, NY, 1995) p. 17.

[2] Kami Watson Huyse, original interview, June 8, 2007.

[3] Brian Oberkirch, "Insights that Matter from Brian Oberkirch," The Buzz Bin, May 1, 2007 (http://www.livingstonbuzz.com/blog/2007/05/01/insights-that-matter-from-brian-oberkirch/).

[4] Steve Rubel, "Blog Search is Dead and Google Killed It", Micropersuasion, http://www.micropersuasion.com/2007/05/blog_search_is_.html.

[5] Don Tapscott and Anthony Williams, Wikinomics, Portfolio Publishing (New York, NY: 2006), p. 80.

[6] Toby Bloomberg, original interview, June 9, 2007.

[7] Mario Sundar, "Face Book Polls: Market Research Meets Social Networks," Marketing Nirvana, June 3, 2007 (http://mariosundar.wordpress.com/2007/06/03/facebook-polls-market-research-meets-social-networks/).

[8] David Meerman Scott, The New Rules of Marketing & PR, John Wiley & Sons, Inc. (Hoboken, New Jersey: 2007), p. 38.

[9] Chris Dorobek, "FCW Insider Chris Dorobek Discusses Federal Blogs and Social Media," The Buzz Bin, June 12, 2007 (http://www.livingstonbuzz.com/blog/2007/06/12/fcw-insider-chris-dorobek-on-federal-social-media/).

[10] Kevin Dugan and Richard Laermer, The Bad Pitch Blog, (http://badpitch.blogspot.com/).

[11] Todd Defren, "Participation is Marketing," PR Squared, May 24, 2007 (http://www.pr-squared.com/2007/05/participation_is_marketing.html).

[12] Rich Becker, Copywrite, Ink., "Ordering Up Ethics: Flogs, Blogs and Posers," July 27, 2007 (http://copywriteink.blogspot.com/2007/07/ordering-up-ethics-flogs-blogs-and.html).

[13] Scott Baradell, "For God's Sake Do Not Try and Tell Us What a Blog Is," Media Orchard, May 2, 2007 (http://www.ideagrove.com/blog2007_05_01_archive.html#2306700750415198097).

[14] GM's Fastlane (http://fastlane.gmblogs.com/).

[15] Alicia Dorset, "Update: Questioning Our Brand Strategy, "GM's Fastlane, June 1 (http://fastlane.gmblogs.com/archives/2007/06/update_question_1.html).

[16] Debbie Weil, "How GM's Fastlane blog was born." BlogWrite for CEOs: The Blog. 6/8/2005. http://blogwrite.blogs.com/blogwrite/2005/06/how_gms_fastlan.html.

[17] Neville Hobson, "An open conversation with General Motors." NevOn. 2/22/2005. http://www.nevon.net/nevon/2005/02/an_open_convers.html.

[18] Shel Holtz, "Weighing in on the Ghost Blogging Debate," A Shel of my Former Self, June 5, 2007 (http://blog.holtz.com/index.php/weblog/comments/weighing_in_on_the_ghost_blogging_debate/).

[19] Scott Baradell, "For God's Sake Do Not Try and Tell Us What a Blog Is," Media Orchard, May 2, 2007 (http://www.ideagrove.com/blog/2007_05_01_archive.html#2306700750415198097).

[20] Charlene Li, New ROI of Blogging Report, The Groundswell, January 25, 2007 (http://blogs.forrester.com/charleneli/2007/01/new_roi_of_blog.html).

[21] We have included a blog roll and list of books at the end of this book to help you in these and other aspects of social marketing media.

22 Darren Rowse, "Does Blog Design Matter In The Early Stages of a Blog," ProBlogger, June 5, 2007 (http://www.problogger.net/archives/2007/06/05/does-blog-design-matter-in-the-early-stages-of-a-blog/).

23 Beth Kanter, "Measuring Your Blogs Outcomes" Beth's Blog, May 2007 (http://beth.typepad.com/beths_blog/2007/05/measuring_your_.html).

24 CBCNet, "Hillary Clinton asks YouTube users to pick campaign song," CBCNet, May 6, 2007 (http://www.cbc.ca/technology/story/2007/05/26/clinton-youtube-song.html).

25 Hillary Clinton, "Pick My Campaign Song: Part 2," Hillary for President, (http://www.youtube.com/watch?v=LClOHUFUC5g&mode=user&search=).

26 Associated Press, "Clinton asks youTube Users for Song Help,"Boston Herald, May 26, 2007 (http://news.bostonherald.com/politics/view.bg?articleid=1003282).

27 Jake Matthews, "10 Helpful Hints for Creating

Strong Web site Content," 10e20, May 1, 2007 (http://www.10e20.com/2007/05/01/10-helpful-hints-for-creating-strong-web-site-content).

28 Teli Adlam, "Make Time for Blogging with a Schedule," The OptiNice Blog, June 4 (http://www.optiniche.com/blog/286/make-time-for-blogging-with-a-schedule/).

29 Bob, "5 Reasons I Unsubscribe from Your Blog," Bob Meets World, June 2, 2007(http://bobmeetsworld.com/5-reasons-i-unsubscribed-from-your-blog/).

Chapter 4
Promotion Within Your Community

Now that you've created strategic value for your community, it's time to let the world know about it. Whether your content is a blog entry, video information, a podcast, an online radio show, or a part of a social network, creating great content makes your entry into new media environments valid and worthy. But a "build it and they shall come" attitude could stop your content from reaching its fullest potential. Additionally, hosting it with an "us vs. them" mentality will immediately segregate the community, thus beginning its demise before it can flourish.

As the social media environment crowds with more and more people, including businesses and organizations trying to participate in their various communities, it creates competition for your community members' attention.

To help attract members of your community to the valuable content created for them, you'll need a community relations program.

While some of these tactics are conventional, they should all be used with the spirit of participation, based on service, relationships, and trust.

The attitude must be one of approaching fellows, rather than generating leads or selling products. Those events—obviously a desired goal—should be considered a by-product of successfully interacting with your community, a result of providing valuable insights and information to them. In essence, help them and they'll help you.

In a guest article on the Successful and Outstanding Bloggers Blog, Hanni Ross writes, "The key message…is *community participation*. The more you give to the community, the more you can expect to get back."[1]

This is the true Zen of social media. Even our outreach must be in the spirit of giving and sharing. Participation must be transparent and it must add value—not just support and comments related to your company, but a general enthusiasm for helping across a spectrum of topics. Whatever your chosen method of community marketing, communicate the value created from the steps taken in Chapter Three. The value represents the strategy, while the outreach mechanisms are really tactics to make you a more prominent member of the community.

The following tactical areas comprise some of the more common ways to interact within different forms of social networks. These general areas range from the simplest to the most complex. Some require detailed experience and learning within the blog world, others require consistent maintenance, and still others are specific campaign-oriented initiatives.

Now Is Gone is not meant to teach business owners and marketing practitioners how to execute all of these tactics. There are plenty of books and blogs that provide how-tos and tips on marketing within social networks, including how to blog, how to optimize your chances for being Dugg, etc. We've included two appendices: The first is a blog roll of cited sources and the second provides a list of books that can help expand tactical and strategic knowledge. *Now Is Gone* means to provide you the information necessary for intelligent leadership, empowering champions for change by teaching you how to build your organization's community via general tactics.

These tactical categories are:

1. Participation is marketing
2. RSS and tag-based blogosphere buzz
3. Social networks
4. Traditional media relations
5. Blogger outreach
6. Social media releases
7. Old tactics

Participation is Marketing

Participation really means more than acting as a member of your community; it means contributing to its success. It goes beyond simply creating great content and value for a community. While that's definitely a big part of an organization's role in this new media world, it is still critical for the entity to do more. They need to participate by commenting on other relevant blogs and sites, talking about issues that matter to the larger community (and not just their business), linking back to other blogs, and participating in the community's related events.

There are many ways to participate, and many contemporary marketing blogs and books discuss these specific tactics. But there's still a strategic ethos to participation that many of these marketing minds fail to realize.

One of the leading minds in the industry, Chris Heuer, tells everyone he meets that participation equates to marketing in online social networks. It's at this very base point that the concept of a business as a member of the community occurs, generating the value of the business owner or member interacting with their customers.[2]

"The reason for [business's] formation was to help people with a specific problem, desire, or need — that the all important intention of contributing to the community by participating in it was their original purpose," said Chris Heurer. "It is this key shift in thinking, returning to the roots of our society and the organization's role in it, that is represented by my simple, snack sized sound byte that *participation is marketing*."[3]

Participation means engaging with your community and communicating. It's the difference between simply showing up and maintaining an active, positive profile. You will build great relationships, you will encourage them to tell you what they need, and your business will thrive because it's helping people. In short, participation attracts customers from your community. These types of customers build more value with relationship-oriented loyalty, as opposed to transactional gratification.[4] This is true of small and large businesses.

SplashCast's Community Participation Case Study

SplashCast, a service that enables anyone to create streaming media 'channels' that combine video, music, photos, narration, text and RSS feeds, hired two experienced social media producers, Marshall Kirkpatrick and Alex Williams, to engage with existing social media communities. Marshall writes blog posts that are accompanied by channels of mixed media content compiled using our company's product. Alex publishes interviews from events using SplashCast.

Through their blog, Marshall and Alex drive traffic to the SplashCast Web site, demonstrate the potential of the company's publishing tool, and ultimately encourage people to sign up as SplashCast publishers themselves. The primary ways that Marshall and Alex worked to build readership for their blog include:

- Daily blogging, not only about company news, but interesting industry news as well. Some of their posts have been deemed interesting enough to receive thousands of visitors from StumbleUpon, for example.

- Sending trackbacks to other blogs, where their posts that are related to others are linked for their readers to discover.

- Leaving thoughtful, value-add-focused comments in response to posts on other blogs, where their names are tagged with the SplashCast site URL.

- Making relevant bloggers central to our product

---

release PR. That strategy led to more than 250 blog mentions within forty-eight hours of SplashCast's launch.

- Attending events and building relationships with other social media producers.

- Using *Twitter* to stay abreast of what other people are doing and keep friends up to date on SplashCast.

- Engagement with and inclusion in relevant topical aggregators. For example, *a Google search of Techmeme.com for SplashCastMedia* brings back 1,400 results and they made 15 appearances on the front page of Digg.

"We find creative ways to participate in conversations of general interest," said Marshall Kirkpatrick. In particular, we let people publish aggregated collections of mixed media, so we watch the news and see what would be interesting to publish collections like this about. When the [Department of Defense] banned social media sites from official networks, we published a channel of videos and photos tagged Iraq in YouTube and Photobucket, for example."

As a result of these and other participation activities, SplashCast had more than 1,000 publishers register for an account at launch. They doubled that in their first month to 2,000 and doubled it again in their second month to more than 4,000. SplashCast player loads are now approaching 5.5 million.

SplashCast demonstrates that participation really is marketing. By being a part of their social network community online, participating in a variety of ways, the community responded when they launched. As a result, their product received significant attention upon launch, and continues to develop traction online.

"Push, broadcast style advertising will probably always dominate the market because reaching for huge numbers is just too tantalizing to give up," said Kirkpatrick. "But a strategy of more authentic communication as the new media producer—on consumers' own turf and terms—offers a real and efficient opportunity to secure at the very least a significant mindshare among market influencers. Plus it feels a lot better than being a traditional marketer."

RSS and Social Network Promotion

Real Simple Syndication, or RSS technology, allows a wide variety of social media users to access your content through a series of mechanisms. RSS strategies are the basic blocking and tackling of garnering a loyal following of community members who regularly read, listen to, or view your content. They don't need to seek you out, instead the content is delivered to them. Interested consumers subscribe to your blog, getting the latest updates via portals that aggregate postings a la Technorati, NewsGator, Google Reader, SplashCast, and many more, or having the entries sent directly to them via e-mail services like FeedBlitz and FeedBurner.

Here are some of the basic RSS strategies suggested by Kim Roach:

- Get a FeedBurner service so people can receive e-mail from you
- Submit your site to RSS directories and content aggregators

- Add a large RSS button to your site
- Have RSS links at the bottom of each content entry
- Offer an e-mail newsletter in addition to RSS. An e-mail newsletter allows you to form a closer relationship with your visitors and picks up those who still aren't comfortable with RSS technology[5]

As important, if not more so, is participation within the larger social bookmarking networks like Digg!, Stumble Upon, del.icio.us, and others. When a company gets an article, video, or other content Dugg, Stumbled Upon, or Newsvined, huge amounts of visitors see the content. This has the potential to create an avalanche effect that can even crash Web servers. Hundreds, even thousands of readers, can visit the content, leveraging the social network for a temporary rush of potential new community members.[6]

The benefits of such an event can include:

- Fresh RSS and newsletter subscribers from visitors
- New links from visitors who like the referrred column
- Digging culture emerges, where more and more successive waves occur. In short, it becomes easier to get recognized in these larger social networks
- Search engine optimization increases

In short, a social network recognition event(s) can work to really increase your community size for the long-haul.[7]

To leverage this effect, a site needs to be optimized effectively. That means bookmarking tags must be visible to readers so they can easily refer your content to their network, and other additional tactics a content creator can deploy to make itself more attractive to these social networks.

The most obvious is to actually participate in the network. By participating you learn what the community wants and likes, and can better meet its needs by creating the content that's most valuable to it. This represents the enduring principle of *Now Is Gone*, build value for your community, and work for them.

Search Media Gurus remind us that *social media is more than Digg and Stumble Upon.* "*Before you apply [Digg optimization techniques]—know your target audience.* If you're targeting Digg, then [implementing] suggestions make sense, but if you understand [that] social media goes well beyond those news type sites, approach the suggestions with caution. In the end, it's all about *knowing your audience.*" Well said. Your community may not be "Diggers," so write for them, not for the thrill of being Dugg.[8]

For a content creator, the general strategic take home on RSS and social network optimization lies in making it easy for potential community members to accept your content into their preferred reading mechanisms. Build it not only so they'll come, but so they'll choose to come back.

Social Networks Can Help

An organization can identify social networks that have pools of community members, like Twitter, Pownce, Facebook or MySpace. Social networks allow an organization to aggregate contacts in groups of self-identified and voluntarily interested parties. In essence, the community members opt in to your network as a friend or follower (or whatever the network's preferred nomenclature is).

Opt-ins don't give a company a license to engage in shameless promotions. It's important to note that they expect an organization to behave according to the principles outlined in the previous two chapters...in short, as a conversational, contributing member of the community.

Within these networks, Internet "friends" are interested in content and developments generated by members within their network. This is true and even expected of companies and entrepreneurs. Friends may be interested in a book, a blog, or an application you are developing. But whatever the initiative may be, organizations should strategically try to share efforts that contribute to the community in some way.

En masse, that means a company or organization can update large subgroups of people about initiatives. For example, on Twitter, the Live Earth initiative used its microblog updates to keep almost 2,000 bloggers apprised of the July 7, 2007 concerts. Here are some sample "Tweets:"

> "Switching between the live earth stages at liveearth.msn.com. Alicia Keys dueting with Keith Urban. Beastie Boys rockin' london.
> <u>12:40 PM July 07, 2007</u>"

> "Rallying up a road crew. Carpool to relieve congestion on your daily ride to work. Americans waste 2.3 billion [gallons] of gas a year in traffic.
> <u>02:27 PM July 06, 2007</u>"[26]

Intelligent companies use periodic calls to action with their community interaction. For example, many corporate social network members reference a blog post, list a wiki on their identity profile, or collaborate with the community on a social media initiative. By bringing community members closer to the organization's primary social media initiative, larger constituencies are built.

Other networks, such as the very popular Facebook, allow organizations to build private groups in which contacts discuss issues. Facebook has designed an open application programming interface so that companies can create applications and introduce them into the social network. If successful in creating value for community members, these applications can create a tremendous groundswell of interest in an organization. At the same time, some applications fail because they don't offer value to the community.

"It's not just about the ability to connect with people," said Brian Solis on a post relating to Facebook. "It's about creating, cultivating, and promoting a strategic online presence and personal brand. Remember, participation is marketing."[27]

Companies and organizations should look at social networks as a way to engage potential community members outside of the confines of a corporate URL. By participating intelligently and building value, a company can create a great conversation with its constituents as well as future customers. Further, they can encourage them to take actions and engage them within the confines of the company's own social media initiative.

Traditional Media Relations

One great way to promote your new media initiative remains the traditional media, who often use well-respected blogs as sources or even the subject of stories. When marketing his new book, *The New Rules of Marketing and PR*, (which describes many of the tactics needed in the new media environment), David Meerman Scott says "if you blog, reporters who cover the space will find you," and "Pitch bloggers, because being covered in important blogs will get you noticed by mainstream media."[9]

Blogs drive information into the spotlight, forcing traditional media to pay attention—or look like they've missed the news, and most importantly the conversation. Blogs are more effective in reaching and inspiring traditional media to react than most PR professionals and wire services combined.

Our experience confirms these facts. Numerous clients have received significant media coverage from their efforts in the new media environment. In 2006, Livingston Communications client, FortiusOne, first became noticed by mainstream media outlets *The Washington Post* and *Information Week* after the blogosphere erupted with chatter about the company's innovative new intelligent maps that displayed vast amounts of data on satellite maps using heat signatures. When asked why FortiusOne was important, the Livingston Communications PR team simply referred the reporters to blogsearch.google.com. The vast amount of new media coverage did the rest of the work.

FutureWorks, a new media agency based in Silicon Valley, uses blogs to spark bigger conversations in traditional media. The company specifically works with emerging technology companies, unknown to the masses. In the realm of social media, FutureWorks uses a combination of social video releases (product overview) on YouTube and blogs to break the Beta availably to the people before reaching out to traditional media. All conversations are documented through del.icio.us bookmarks, and in turn are shared with reporters and analysts to convey public support and perceived value.

In the entertainment business, artists today are using social media to generate momentum, support and a loyal fan base forcing labels to compete for their contract. The press react in a similar way, viewing "louder" conversations as the next big thing.

Numerous journalists use blogs as sources, from world renowned organizations like the BBC and *The Washington Post,* to niche trade magazines. In 2005, a new study by Euro RSCG/Columbia University showed that more than 51 percent of journalists use blogs regularly, and 28 percent rely on them to help in their day-to-day reporting duties.[10] "I regard the blogosphere as a source of criticism that must be listened to and as a source of information that can be used," said Paul Reynolds, World Affairs Correspondent, BBC.[11]

When the media recognizes a social media effort—whether it is a blog, YouTube, a social network or other new media initiative—there is a sudden burst of attention to that effort. The blog (or other form of new media) is recognized as a credible source of information, and naturally people that read the article and find it interesting will check out the new media form cited.

Then the content creators' continued participatory effort with its community combined with a savvy RSS strategy can be used to grow its community. Return reader-ship, a larger community, and enhanced brand reputation are the great results of successful media coverage of your new media effort. So be intelligent. When you know a story will be written, leverage the opportunity with fresh, relevant content and intelligent RSS strategies.

Outreach: Pitching to New Media Outlets

There's much debate about communicating directly with bloggers. Frankly, this is a very dangerous tactic for novices just engaging in the new media world, and a debate occurred on the merit of including this tactical area. However, because so many people are bent on pitching bloggers (or other content creators), this section discusses this type of tactic, provides some general guidelines, and serves as a stern warn-ing. This of all of the tactical areas represents the most danger to your effort, and should not be taken lightly.

The classic marketing mistake here remains treating bloggers like traditional media outlets. New media content creators do not have any obligation to "report" or field inquiries, they don't have to write up a review of your product (even if you comp them something), and a great majority distrust traditional public relations tactics. Con-sider the most successful tactic to date, which involves bribing bloggers with free stuff—dubbed with "blogola" by *The Wall Street Journal*.[12] This type of push puts PR people in a carpetbagger role.

Specific tactics will continue to evolve in this realm as bloggers and social networks determine how they want to be communicated to. When strong social network relationships are not in play, news that may be of interest to a community cannot be communicated naturally and virally. This puts an organization or company in a position of weakness, as it forces marketing to promote initiatives rather than attract attention. Social media is not conducive to this kind of promotion.

When there is a strong social network strategy in play, members of the community feel tied to the organization's efforts, and if they believe in the organization, are often willing to help promote it. A dialogue already exists, so it's OK to tell your social network about an exciting new development...so long as it's of interest to them, too. The Splashcast team's intelligent dialoging with the blogging community before the company's launch is a great example of engaging a community in this manner.

That being said, if an organization must promote in an outbound fashion, our experience demonstrates that a very simple pitch must be drawn up for new media outlets that's very customized to each particular blog. Any pitch must be about the new media outlet's interests/content direction, and must provide value to them by providing some sort of useful facts or information. That can include early trials of products or services, but be wary, as this does not guarantee positive write-ups. In fact, if the information is poor, you can expect a negative write-up. Use of only one URL should be included, pointing the outlet back to more information in one central location (such as a social media release). No pitch should overtly demand or request pickup, instead providing an "FYI." The pitch is usually submitted as a tip via a Web form on the site, or e-mailed to the blogger *IF* their site invites tips. Once you send your pitch, let it go. Period. That means do not follow up or harass the blogger/content creator, at all. Pressure equals bad write-ups about your organization.

If there's no pick-up or interest, take it as a sign that your company just engaged in shameless promotion instead of creating value for your community, and start your new media strategy over. And be happy you didn't get slammed by one of the bloggers. Begin again by building value for the community instead of trying to exploit its members by pitching them.

"If a marketer is bent on 'exploiting' anything, it will likely bite him in the ass," said Todd Defren, principal at SHIFT Media. "That was *always* the case, of course, but in the Social Media world, the difference is that you'll be [found] out more quickly, and the 'punishment' can be [harsher] and more long-lasting. My advice is to start any Social Media campaign by listening and quietly participating (as a user, not a marketer): This is the best way to 'find the line;' to get a true sense for community standards."[13]

The Social Media Release

Outbound communications from public relations teams often includes a central document for information communication, conventionally a news release. With the evolution of media has come the evolution of the news release. Just like successful corporate entities incorporation of community value within their social media outreach, the news release has begun its evolution towards a second generation incarnation. The social media release reinvents news to be much more palatable to a variety of audiences, including journalists and interested new media content creators.

Over the past seven years, the news release has become a weaker and weaker form of promotion. This is particularly true when a business or its agency issues a release that has diminished or no news value to the media or associated communities. News is something that's new, and as media are dedicated to business trends or events of significance that their communities care about, they use filters to tune out the increasingly larger number of corporate releases thrown at them. Thus, the value of news releases are diminished. Though the press release does have some search engine optimization and secondary direct community outreach value, its old incarnation is no longer optimized for ultimate results.

In an article she wrote for the online marketing community MarketingProfs, Sally Saville Hodge writes, "…the reality is that the press release is pretty much dead as a piece of the strategic communications arsenal. Think about it. As a society, we've gone from the era of mass production, mass merchandising and mass marketing, to one where customization is king… As far as most reporters and editors are concerned, they are overproduced, they lack differentiation, they generally aren't relevant and the vast majority just aren't worthy of coverage."[14]

Enter new media, and the great amount of content being created in blogs, podcast and video networks, and then the dissemination and discussion of them via social networks. Suddenly there are many more ways to communicate with a community. But the news release doesn't work for new media communities either, for the same reason that traditional media increasingly don't use press releases as a primary source.

Originally created by Todd Defren of SHIFT Media, the social media release combines the best elements of new media and significantly streamlines the valuable elements of the news release.[15] While there are many variants of the original template, social media releases are an attempt to provide these communities with information that matters to them.

The social media release provides new media community members dynamic information, including a statement of value, additional sources and multimedia content (podcast, video, graphics, etc.). Readers are provided social media methods of publishing via network tags, and can use these elements independently or as a whole, according to their tastes. And media members like them, too.

In an interview for this book, Todd Defren said, "The strength of the SMNR is its ability to democratize access to the content and multimedia with which we tell stories on the Web. Anyone can rip content from the SMNR and use it within their own publishing forum, as they see fit. This serves to widely disseminate news, and also gives consumers and publishers more input on the evolution of the newsmaker's story and brand.

"In addition, the SMNR creates more dialogue and context around each news item. Done right, the SMNR becomes a blog post, which lives on its own microsite, with moderated comments, trackbacks, etc. that show the interplay of the news with the news consumer."[16]

The combination of advanced push techniques, and the well crafted tags and social network pulls creates a new dynamic marketing mechanism. This next generation press release is much more valuable to its audiences, is community-centric, enables widespread dissemination, and creates multiple methods of pulling in community members who may be interested in your service, product, or ideas.[17]

Coca-Cola new media agency crayon used a social media release to announce Virtual Thirst. "It's a no brainer in today's world that you have to go beyond just blitzing out the traditional press release through the usual channels," said project lead C.C. Chapman. "A social media press release formats the information so only the best nuggets are showcased. The bulleted format makes it quick to scan and grab the parts that you need to run with. Plus, with one click to audio, photos, videos, and other forms of media, it makes it extremely friendly to bloggers and podcasters who want to write about it."[18]

In a blog entry dedicated to social media releases, Online Marketing Blog writer Lee Odden said, "By optimizing your media release and adding social media, you can increase the distribution channels and take advantage of increased visibility to demand driven traffic."[19] Clearly, as online media forms become increasingly predominant, media releases will continue to evolve and meet this new communities' needs.

Social Media Success Story: Virtual Thirst

Coca Cola launched a Second Life initiative, labeled "Virtual Thirst," by using a different approach than the traditional island purchase, building an edifice, and hoping residents will stop by for a visit. Working with the crayon agency, Coca-Cola opted to break into the 3D metaverse by getting out amongst the population.

The competitive effort between residents to design a Coca-Cola vending machine that dispenses an experience (as opposed rather than a can or bottle of Coke). A social media release was used to announce the initiative and draw in interested bloggers and media.[20]

Bloggers, "in-world" media, and mainstream media were invited to attend the event, which was held on Crayonville Island. The crayon venue hosted the Virtual Thirst pavilion. crayon recruited an advisory panel of Second Life residents to make sure the effort was in sync with the metaverse's culture. And Coca-Cola did not "deploy" the winning machine when it was finally built; the corporation simply made it available at no cost to residents who wanted one. During the Second Life launch event, one blogger in attendance told Shel Holz that that the effort was like a classic "How to do social media right."[21]

Other dimensions of the competition included a range of ways to submit entries, such as YouTube videos and postings to MySpace profiles, development of a MySpace profile, and uploading a video of prototypes to YouTube. The grand prize was a trip to San Francisco, where the winner witnessed Millions of Us, one of the premier builders of Second Life structures and objects, turn the design into a Second Life reality.[22]

"The majority of the writing was of a positive nature," said crayon project leader, C.C. Chapman. "People seemed to be refreshed that Coke decided to strategically go small instead of just building another island that would turn into a ghost town. Even some of the harshest critics of big brands coming into Second Life wrote positive responses about it.

"There were some very vocal critics and critiques of the program but Coke was smart enough to see and listen to crayon's encouragements to go back out and engage in the conversation with these people," added Chapman. "A video diary response was recorded and posted to YouTube that answered the major questions/criticisms. People were not expecting that, and it was fun to read their reactions. I liked seeing people that we thought might attack the program actually speak positively of the effort even if they didn't like some parts of it."[23]

Leverage Your Current Marketing Activities

There's a cliché in the advertising business that you need to touch a customer seven different times (this number varies depending on the source) through a variety of mechanisms to get them to act. Regardless of the actual number, it's important to note the use of different media forms to promote your social media effort. For example, several Super Bowl and Oscars ads in 2007 invited viewers to their Web site, and in some cases, the ads were selected or created by participants within the company's social media community.[24]

These advertisers knew that social media users also access information through a variety of mechanisms, so they communicated through an integrated outreach effort. Some very simple and obvious ways to promote a blog or other new media initiatives include:

- E-mail signatures
- Prominent link on main Web site
- E-mail or letter of introduction to existing contact databases
- Direct mail
- Provide links in newsletters promising related, value-added content
- Include URL in business cards and stationary
- Advertisements
- Inclusion within corporate brochures and collateral

All of these will make current new media users aware of your content. If they are somewhat curious, there's a great opportunity to start a dialogue and build a more loyal community. You may even migrate your current consumers of traditional media communications to new media.

Zaadz, an online social network for the alternative spiritual community seeking to "change the world" (*www.zaadz.com*), uses print publications via traditional advertising and their subscriber lists to reach ideal customers. In an interview with *What is Enlightenment?* magazine, Zaadz founder, Brian Johnson said, "It's a group of people that is pretty self-identified as readers of *What Is Enlightenment?* magazine, readers of *Shambhala Sun* or *Yoga Journal* or *Science of Mind*, etc. We get so many responses from people who read our first ad, or a letter from me, and come to the site and say, 'Finally, I feel like I'm home.'"[25] Zaadz keeps their potential audience with a great amount of dynamic content ranging from interaction with other Zaadsters and brick and mortar events to a team blog and podcasts.

While not all traditional media consumers will migrate to your new content and the value you've created for them, some will. Migration towards new media is inevitable as the form becomes more dominant. And by helping or making your community aware of your organization's effort, you continue to build value in your peering and outreach efforts with an even larger community.

Parting Thoughts

With the social media environment becoming more crowded every day, a communications program needs to reach social media users and interest them in the company's foray into the field. This program should be tailored in a community-based method, trying to give something of value to the users. In turn, they will return the favor.

There are seven outreach tactical areas that can be employed, including looking at participation as marketing, RSS and tag based blogosphere buzz, social networks, traditional media relations, blogger outreach, social media releases, and old tactics. Chapter four focuses on how a company can use these seven areas to attain exposure online.

Participation is Marketing

Participation means engaging with the company's community. By participating, a company attracts customers from the community. When a company is involved in this area, the customers tell the company what they need or want, and the ensuing dialogue fosters a true relationship. Community members value the two-way relationship they have with the company, and have more loyalty to the brand, rather than simply receiving a service and being satisfied.

RSS and Social Network Promotion

Real Simple Syndication or RSS, is a way for a company to connect with its most loyal readers or users. RSS technologies allow regular visitors not to have to seek out a blog or site, their RSS portal gives them a link to new content, or a program like FeedBurner e-mails the content directly.

Additionally, leveraging and working of hits within large social networks, like Digg and Stumble Upon, can help a company increase its RSS readership. Content creators should optimize their site to capture readers during these events.

Social Networks

Social Networks that feature opt-in friends or followers can be great ways to engage sub-communities outside of a corporate social media initiative. By building value for these contacts in a participation-oriented, value-building manner, organizations can intelligently build an extended community of brand loyalists. Further, an organization can encourage community members to take actions and engage within the confines of the organization's own social media initiative.

Traditional Media Relations

A growing number of journalists use blogs as sources, from worldwide sources like the BBC, to smaller trade or niche magazines. When mainstream media reports on a social media campaign, it creates excitement and credibility. With a diligent content creator, this media coverage can yield a large growth in return readership, community, and brand reputation.

Outreach: Pitching to New Media Outlets

This type of communication is the most hazardous of all the tactics explored for those that are new to social media. When communicating with bloggers directly, a company must be wary not to make a pitch-type message, but rather an FYI with valuable information for the community. If there is no interest, the company should take time to review and revise the outreach strategy to better understand what information would provide the community value.

The Social Media Release

Press releases simply do not influence or get coverage in today's media environment. Many in the media find them overproduced and not relevant or worthy of reporting. The social media news release morphs the information typically contained in a press release into, in effect, a blog post. Unique content like podcasts or video is used, as well as information that is of real value to the community, with additional sources provided. Both new and old media have taken a liking to this type of corporate communication.

Leverage Your Current Marketing Activities

Different forms of media should be used to pull a social media campaign. Many television ads encourage interested persons to visit their Web site, some companies even have users within their social media community create ads for them. Leverage your traditional marketing efforts in full to build a social media community. Migratory users will grow in number as new media continues to expand its presence within the communications space.

Notes

[1] Hanni Ross, "Building Readership: Community Participation," Successful and Outstanding Bloggers (http://www.successful-blog.com/writing/building-traffic-community-participation/).

[2] Chris Heuer, "Participation is Marketing," The Future of Communities (http://www.futureofcommunities.com/2007/03/12/participation-is-marketing/).

[3] Ibid.

[4] Ibid.

[5] Kim Roach, "101 Steps to Become a Better Blogger," Lifehack.org (http://www.lifehack.org/articles/technology/101-steps-to-becoming-a-better-blogger.html).

[6] Kami Huyse, "Harnessing the Digg Event" Communications Overtone (http://overtonecomm.blogspot.com 2007_04_01_archive.html).

[7] Darren Rows, "How to Build a Digg Culture," ProBlogger (http://www.problogger.net/archives/2006/12/27/how-to-build-a-digg-culture-on-your-blog/).

[8] Li Evans, "Social Media Isn't Just Digg and Stumble Upon," Search Media Gurus (http://www.searchmarketinggurus.com/search_marketing_gurus/2007/05/social_media_is.html).

[9] David Meerman Scott, "Online PR Expert Reveals the New Rules of PR and How to Reach the Media," PRWeb, May 21, 2007 (http://www.emediawire.com/releases/2007/5/emw522206.htm).

[10] Steve Rubel, "Study: Majority of Journalists Blog,"

Micropersuasion (http://www.micropersuasion.com/2005/06/
study_majority_.html).

[11] Paul Reynolds, "Bloggers: An Army of Irregulars," BBC, February
9, 2006 (http://news.bbc.co.uk/1/hi/world/4696668.stm).

[12] Brooks Barnes, "To Create Buzz, TV Networks Try a Little
'Blogola,'" WSJ.com, May 15, 2007 (http://online.wsj.com/article/
SB117919274561702788.html?mod=djemITP).

[13] Geoff Livingston, "PR Squared's Todd Defren Talks About Social
Media Release," The Buzz Bin, (http://www.livingstonbuzz.com/
blog/2007/05/17/pr-squareds-todd-defren-talks-about-social-
media-releases).

[14] Sally Seville Hodge, "The Press Release Is Dead," Marketing Profs,
http://www.marketingprofs.com/5/hodge3.asp.

[15] Todd Defren, "The Social Media Release Debuts," PR Squared,
http://www.pr-squared.com/2006/05/
the_social_media_press_release.html.

[16] Geoff Livingston, "PR Squared's Todd Defren Talks About Social
Media Release," The Buzz Bin, (http://www.livingstonbuzz.com/
blog/2007/05/17/pr-squareds-todd-defren-talks-about-social-
media-releases).

[17] Lee Odden, "Social Media Release Optimization," Online Marketing
Blog (http://www.toprankblog.com/2006/11/social-media-release-
optimization/).

[18] C.C. Chapman, original interview, June 17, 2007.

[19] Ibid.

[20] Shel Holz, "Coca-Cola's Community Approach to Second Life," a
shel of my former self (http://blog.holtz.comindex.php
coca_colas_community_approach_to_second_life/).

[21] Ibid.

[22] Ibid.

[23] C.C. Chapman, original interview.

[24] Amy Stodgehill, "Got an Idea for a Green Ad Campaign," Green Options
(http://www.greenoptions.com/blog/2007/03/03/
got_an_idea_for_a_green_ad_campaign_send_it_to_yahoo).

[25] Carter Phipps and Andrew Cohen, "This Revolution Will Be Digitized," What is Enlightenent?, Issue 36, April-June 2007, 120.

[26] Live Earth, "LiveEarth070707," July 6-7, 2007, http://twitter.com/LiveEarth070707

[27] Brian Solis, "Facebook is the Online Hub for Connected Professionals," PR 2.0, August 6, 2007, http://www.briansolis.com/2007/08/facebook-is-online-hub-for-connected.html

Chapter 5
The Future Cometh:
Integrating Social Media Principles
Into Marketing

A s this is a primer for executives on how to begin engaging in social media, it is important to discuss the future impact of this dynamic trend. It's inevitable that a sweeping societal change will greatly impact corporations...not just as a specific marketing tactic, but marketing as a whole. In some cases—particularly for consumer centric activities—marketing's approach can impact the entire organization's business operations, from storefront interaction to backend customer support.

This chapter will discuss several aspects of how social media will continue to impact organizations. Specifically, we will discuss:

- The participation is marketing approach affect on marketing strategy

- Impact on PR
- Impact on Advertising
- Impact on Other Marketing Forms
- Technology's Continued Impact on Social Media

Participation Affects All Marketing

The "Participation is Marketing" concept impacts marketing minds more than any other aspect of social media. This user-generated phenomenon changes the entire approach of most marketing professionals, forcing them to engage communities by their rules. The most likely impact of social media will be the viral spread of "community engagement principles" to other disciplines within the marketing arsenal.

"[The future of marketing]'s a mashup of new media and traditional media—all with the common goal of engaging people and influencers on their terms," said co-contributor Brian Solis in a post dubbed the "Future of Communications." "...by listening, reading, and participating, corporate marketing will be smarter and more approachable than ever before. This is how we humanize brands, create loyalty, and earn customers' business."[1]

Increased usage of social media forms will be fueling this shift. In many ways, this change will be fueled by the inevitable passing of time; as older generations move out of the work place and social media usage increases across wider demographics. This usage will vary widely from member networks, like Facebook and Second Life, to evolved forms of user generated content, like Twitter and verticalized blog networks. Many of the future forms of social media have yet to emerge.

"I'm convinced the social influence of My Space and similar identity networks will continue to expand rapidly," said Kipp Monroe, Chief Creative Officer at White and Partners, and a producer of Super Bowl ads for Budweiser and Miller. "By 2025 every man, woman and child in America (and most of the developed world) will belong to some sort of network community. And, of course, wherever eyeballs travel, advertising follows. A great deal of attention will be paid by marketers to these types of network communities."[2]

Demand for user generated content, social networks, and other forms of participatory content has continued to evolve. The social media phenomenon is expected to continue to increase dramatically.[3] With it, feedback and discussion of products will be increasingly important for companies. Social media's impact has already spread well beyond age brackets into vertical industries.

According to Sys-Con magazine, as of June 2007, 42.6 percent of IT professionals rely on user generated content to make enterprise purchasing decisions, more than any other media form.[4] The resulting impact on technology companies is noticeable. At the June 2006 Best Practices in Corporate Communications New Media Summit, Cisco executive Dan Sheinman revealed that Cisco's Web traffic has completely switched from static Web pages to blog views and RSS feeds. Blog posts outstripped RSS Feeds and podcasts 9 to 1, and outpaced traditional Web page views 45 to 1 through the third quarter of 2007.[5]

This overspill is already growing beyond the technology marketplace to other vertical markets, such as real estate, aviation, government, professional services and more. Companies that continue to market with a strict focus on generating leads, dictating the message and solely achieving corporate goals will find communities that resist their efforts. In fact, the market will come to distrust them.

"Most marketers, for a long time, have had the luxury of delivering a message one way, top down, and they knew that people were going to listen, and some were going to be influenced by what they saw or what they heard," said Shel Holtz, co-podcaster and renowned author of *The Hobson and Holtz Report*. "We have seen fewer and fewer organizations able to continue to hold the public's trust as trust shifts to the peer space. The reason trust's shifting is because the original sources of information, business, mainstream media, and government, have egregiously violated that trust on a number of occasions in the past several years."[6]

"Consumers have already become less tolerant of traditional media and 'hard sell' creative tactics," said Kipp Monroe. "That's one of the reasons advertising isn't working. It's the marketers themselves who cling to the traditional channels and in-your-face content. It will be those marketers with products targeted at younger segments who will be the first to evolve to a more culturally astute selling strategy."[7]

As 20th century "one-way" marketing initiatives increasingly fail, companies will be forced to address their strategic approach towards marketing in order to survive. Innovation will occur, creating more community-centric initiatives. Strategies and language will shift from baiting audiences for leads, to encouraging community participation and involvement in a brand's activity. Whether it's Coke or Boeing, customers will want their needs and wants reflected in their chosen product's growth, and to do that, companies will need to become engrained as part of the community. And that means researching, listening to and becoming a part of the community through its chosen social media forms.

"All aspects of what marketers are doing now will change," said Scott Baradell, President of Idea Grove. "It starts with the increasing importance of a traditional component of marketing programs: Researching your customer. It is more important now than ever to know and understand your customer, and it's also more important to listen to your customer. Customers today *expect* to be understood; they *expect* to be listened to. Just get involved in social networks, blogs, etc., and you can learn most of what you need to know—all of which can be applied to your 'traditional' marketing program, as well as what you're doing on the Web."[8]

The impact has already begun to affect the way marketers approach their communities, with user-generated Super Bowl ads, public relations pros engaging bloggers (successfully and unsuccessfully), direct mail seeking to engage targets in new media, and vice versa. Not only will tactics integrate, but approaches will change too, becoming oriented in tone towards what the end-user and community as a whole wants, and within their preferred communication mechanisms.

As marketers come to understand their constituencies' needs they will be more responsive, engaging them in unforeseen ways. Whether it's at a store, on the phone with a customer service representative or online through value added content, these forms are being increasingly dominated and impacted by social media. And the social media initiatives often don't look like the same-old hype with a premium offer. That's because as marketing strategy shifts towards a participation approach, the tactics naturally evolve, too. They become community oriented.

Scott Baradell's Idea Grove has already incorporated a participation approach to several of its campaigns. One of their clients, eDrugSearch.com, created the *Healthcare 100*, a power ranking of the many fragmented healthcare blogs that adds cohesion to the industry. The Healthcare 100 is offering a better sense of community to this corner of the blogosphere, and eDrugSearch.com reaps the benefits of being noticed and recognized for its contribution.[9]

Another example is Black Star, a 70-year-old brand in the photography business that needed to be introduced to a younger, Web-savvy audience in anticipation of its planned Web-based service offerings. Working with Idea Grove, Black Star created a blogzine that adds value to the photography community by attracting world-class photographers, the world's leading authority in the stock photography business, and others, to contribute articles and insights. The investment in the community is dramatically increasing Black Star's brand awareness and positive brand associations with the company's new target audiences.[10]

"Social media's really about serving your customer better," said Kami Watson Huyse. "We need to remember that we are talking directly to the people that we serve. Social media better allows us to return to the true meaning of public relations, which is a two-way, mutually beneficial relationship between an organization and its stakeholders."[11]

As companies strategically shift to participation, their users and their community will come to better embrace them. The relationship will change, and in many ways the 21st century customer relationship will be a stronger one because it's now a two-way conversation. This type of marketing lends itself to creating trust, which in turn creates sales opportunities. And in the end, that is the heart of marketing.

"Where social media really shines is creating relationships which are the first steps to customer acquisition and the reinforcement of customer retention," said Diva Marketing blogger, Toby Bloomberg. "Taking an active role in creating a dialogue with customers about issues that they care about, at the moment in time when they care about those concerns, is the heart of new media marketing."[12]

SeaWorld Case Study:
Social Media as Corporate Outreach

Anheuser-Busch (A-B), owner of SeaWorld Adventure Parks, has experimented with selected forms of social media within its corporate outreach programs. Webcasts of quarterly reports have been offered on their official Web site since mid-2006, and within its Letter to Shareholders in the annual report for 2006, CEO August Busch IV wrote that the company "will continue developing innovative marketing and dedicating resources to make sure our core brands...continue to resonate with an increasingly diverse consumer base."[13]

Within three month of this letter, Anheauser-Busch launched Bud.T.V. and also used social media in an innovative Sea World marketing campaign. Specifically, SeaWorld integrated numerous social media components into the site and won over bloggers by treating them like trusted journalists.

Consultants Kami Watson Huyse and Josh Hallett publicized the opening of the Journey to Atlantis Water Rollercoaster at their San Antonio location. To jump start social media coverage, Huyse and Hallett selected three bloggers to attend the media day along with members of the local American Coaster Enthusiasts chapter (ACE) to ride JTA before its public opening.[14]

Flickr, YouTube, and Veoh components were used to build awareness and link people back to the Journey to Atlantis (JTA) site. Bloggers within relevant subject areas, such as rollercoaster enthusiasts, could easily post these Web assets on their blog or site, which encourages participation and feedback from readers.

Video was also used. A preview day for SeaWorld employees and families two days before the JTA opening yielded a POV video post the next day. Within the Web site there is a 'Share' section, which allows visitors of JTA to post photos or videos of their experiences.[15]

JTA opened May 14th, and as of May 18th, received 10 reviews on the blogosphere with 3 more pending. Some were lukewarm, as was the case with themeparkinsider.com, but others were glowing, such as thrillride.com and lagesse.org (Stuffleufagus).[16] Most of the comments that had a negative tone were more directed at the fact that the ride does not look intense. Huyse responded to many of these comments, and others, trying to make readers aware that JTA was designed as a more family oriented coaster.

Within a week of opening there were 43 links regarding SeaWorld initiated by the JTA campaign, 12 positive blog posts written about the JTA campaign, and 26 positive blog posts, vlogs, and podcasts about the ride itself. Within a 3 week period, Veoh and Flickr reported a total combined video and picture view count of 14,882, Google analytics reported nearly 10 thousand page views, and Technorati yielded 41 blogs linking to SeaWorldCoasters. Feedburner was also used to track the RSS feed distribution, but experienced only limited success. 19 users subscribed, with 2 receiving the feed via e-mail.

A Technorati search revealed that many, non-coaster enthusiast, personal bloggers have posted positively about their experience on JTA. Many of these bloggers have children, and with this being one of the few thrill rides accessible to the whole family, bloggers enjoy the prospect of a roller coaster they can ride with their kids.

Impact on Public Relations

Integration throughout the marketing department will become increasingly important. As various marketing functions try to grasp their community's new needs and preferred communication methods, marketing departments and functions have to work together. When one marketing form has a message of community and the other dictates value, buyers will become confused, and in some cases, may see the community effort as disingenuous.

"In an offline world, marketing and PR are separate departments with different people and skill sets, but this is not the case on the Web," said David Meerman Scott in his new book, *The New Rules of Marketing and PR*. "And when a buyer is researching your product category by using a search engine, does it really matter if the first exposure is a hit on your Web site, or a news release your organization sent, or a magazine article, or a post on your blog? I'd argue that it does not matter."[18]

Assuming social media marketing principles spread to the entire marketing department's strategic approach, the biggest shift in the actual marketing department will be the increased reliance upon public relations. *Webster's Dictionary* defines PR as "Relations with [the] general public as through publicity; specifically, those functions of a corporation, organization, etc. concerned with attempting to create favorable public opinion for itself."[19]

Social media is at the heart of the text book definition of public relations. That means PR will need to execute campaigns that mean something to communities of buyers and users, instead of the current short-sighted focus on getting media coverage. PR practitioners must transition to listening and understanding stakeholders on their terms, in addition to building relationships with reporters and analysts.

"As long as the company can keep their stakeholder in mind as the primary goal of their communications and marketing effort, then you are going to do things that are in the interest of those stakeholders," said Kami Watson Huyse. "Social media just gives a company an opportunity to 'be real.'"[20]

Jeremy Pepper was one of several prominent PR bloggers who discussed Cisco successfully transitioning its outreach to social media. "[Cisco] made a bet on community—communities for third parties, the publishers' demand to have these things on their Web site," said Jeremy Pepper. "Traditional marketing is very challenged because the tools—print, T.V., radio—are all challenged. The early adopters are not participating in traditional media as much as they used to. PR is the new vehicle for companies to speak to the audience—we are media/content providers/developers, and we can speak directly to consumers."[21]

Putting PR in charge of social media in its own right presents issues. To succeed, public relations professionals need to adapt to the new world. PR practitioners are known for several faults: Many never read targeted publications mastheads or reporters' prior stories. How can they understand their customer if they don't read their blogs?

And then there's the spin element. There's a need for honest, factual participation in social media in order to facilitate a trusting conversation with the community. Spin ends up creating negative traction in new environments, and as such, builds a negative brand image. PR practitioners who rely on spin instead of substance to create positive coverage will suffer terrible results in a new environment.

Many practitioners have been extremely resistant to social media. They are resisting the new rules of PR and marketing.[22] As a result, they fail to bring their companies and clients into the world of new media. Or worse, they use the old rules of PR on social media content creators, causing fiascos like the Nikon D80 campaign. In this particular instance, 50 bloggers received a Nikon D80 from the company's PR firm MWW for 6 months of free use with no obligation to blog. This is a very traditional public relations tactic for magazines and newspapers, but many of the bloggers took this as an offensive attempt at bribery and slammed Nikon on their blogs.[23]

"I guarantee you that's not the conversation Nikon wanted," said Shel Holtz. "It's not like reaching out to media... You have to reach out individually. That's a whole different ballgame and there are PR agencies, even the world's largest in Fleishman-Hillard, looking for social media consultants."[24]

The great challenge of reform, evolution and adoption lays before the PR industry. If public relations professionals cannot adapt, companies will need to seek out social media-savvy professionals and consultants. And PR practitioners that fail to adapt will likely need to seek out new careers. This practice-wide challenge may be the most important social media challenge that can impact the well-being of companies and professionals.

At the same time, it's important to note that progress is occurring. "The era of online interactivity started to establish itself years ago, but only last year did the skeptics start to move off of their 'this fad, too, will pass' comments," said Erik Eggertson on his Common Sense PR blog. "If the Ragans, the IABCs and the Melcrums of the world are spreading the gospel, social media has long ago moved past a fad."[25]

Impact on Advertising

The next most likely candidate for sweeping change

must be the advertising industry. Traditional print and T.V. advertising's decline in recent years has coincided with the rise of social media, in part because users stopped believing what their vendors told them. There are great barriers to advertising because of social media, including trust and privacy.[26]

At the same time, in 2005, advertising agencies that saw drops in traditional advertising media buys shifted towards marketing services for the new world. This has accelerated over the past year and a half as social media has taken off. Businesses increased their total spending on creative dollars into alternative marketing forms, from games and social media, to store experiences and cell phone campaigns.[27]

The significant change has been noticeable with great campaigns, like Coke's Virtual Thirst and Doritos user generated Super Bowl ads, to bombs like Bud.T.V. and untested social networks like Sprite Yard. Regardless of form, major innovation continues to occur in creative shops across America.[28]

Where advertising will go remains to be seen. Is user generated content a novelty, an addition, or the future? Will watering down creative via focus groups become less prevalent? One thing that has been clear is a reinvestment into actual content creativity versus production of the same old 30-second spots.[29] Instead of conveying corporate dogma, agencies are refocusing on their communities of interest and working to build content that excites them.

"I think there's going to have to be some sort of a social media dimension to a lot of the advertising that goes on out there and you're starting to see some of this," said

Shel Holtz. "T.V. commercials now invite you to submit content, for example, or go to a site where you are going to find a greater level of interactivity or involvement with the audience, or what Jay Rosen calls 'the people formally known as the audience.'"[30]

"I have a hunch that the years ahead will be very exciting from a creative standpoint, as well as a from a media view," said Kipp Monroe. "Creative content that does resonate with the culture and cuts through will be in big demand. Call it an online renaissance. I can't wait to see how what we call advertising will look 20 years from now."[31]

It's clear that if advertising will succeed, it needs to better integrate into social media. The thirty second spot, the static full page ad, the banner ad, and the 60 second radio spot are media forms that have been relegated ineffective by new media users. Specifically, they won't tolerate the forced message and the demand on their attention spans. The advanced consumer of media services won't blindly accept messaging, and will demand value.

Thus, advertisers and marketers in general are forced to innovate and integrate into social media…and they may fail, too. Consumers are really going to decide what will and will not be accepted. Smart companies will tap into network and content providers who track what content users are reading, and create, targeting the type and delivery of their ads.

A last thought on advertising: Generation Y reads and plays with content differently. Content will need to reflect their usage patterns and expectations intelligently to provide greater value. Value is the key to success, and thus contributing to the community through advertising may be the path of least resistance.[32]

Impact on Other Marketing Forms

Moving forward to marketing and branding in general, it is likely that the continued advent of social media will create a fusion of voices contributing to branding efforts. In this Wiki-type of environment, users, brand experts, consultants, companies and agencies will collectively collaborate to forge a great marketing scene. This new environment will be fueled by passion, excitement, and the ongoing relationships the social media seems to inspire. This is already happening with a project called BrandingWire where brand experts are working together on a different project every month.[33]

"What if the way the analysis, research, and experience deployed happened simultaneously," said Valeria Maltoni. "Each version would contain a recommendation from a different angle. As diverse as your customer base, and covering so many more ideas."[34]

Integrating social media principles and concepts into other aspects of marketing seems like a natural course, but in many ways the impact is less direct for these tactics in comparison to PR and advertising. In some cases, like direct mail and database marketing, social media really represents an evolution of the form involving one to one contact from companies with community members.

Traditional marketing forms can be tied to social media, extending and promoting initiatives to users and communities on a one-to-one basis. If there is a negative blog comment or post, customer relations can reach out to the disgruntled buyer and resolve the issue. The trouble for marketers and social media will be innovating and exploring the limitless possibilities that the new interactive environment creates for them.[35]

"The future of marketing integrates traditional and social media elements," said Brian Solis. "Remember, the future of communications introduces sociology into the marketing strategy. The technology is just that, technology. The tools will change. The networks will evolve. Mediums for distributing content will grow."[36]

Perhaps that's the problem with forecasting the future of marketing. In many ways, social media opportunities have been created by technology. And as technologies' impact on communications continues to evolve and become increasingly universal throughout our lives, social media and marketing as a whole will continue to evolve. Thus, it would not be fair to continue a conversation without looking at technology and its accelerating impact on marketing.

Technology's Social Media Future

Cisco CEO John Chambers; Motorola CEO Ed Zander; Vice Chairman Bob Wright, GE's lead executive for NBC Universal; Verizon CEO Ivan Seidenberg; and AT&T's CEO and Chairman Randall Stephenson gathered together in mid-June 2007 for NXTComm, the telecommunications industry's leading North American show. There they talked about their companies' social media strategies and hopes.

The reality behind telecom and technology giants is

that in many ways these many voices—handsets, infrastructure, network providers and content creators—are all
in the same boat. They don't know what's coming next,
but they do know that we're at the tip of the iceberg.
They've lost control of the traffic and content viewed on
their networks, equipment and servers.[37]
Social media has been fueled by a dynamic, increasingly open application environment thanks to the widespread adoption application programming interfaces (API),
the open source ethos, and incredible amounts of bandwidth. More than 50 percent of Americans have broadband technology, and suddenly they can stream audio and
video, upload massive photo albums, create dynamic content and share it with social networks.[38] Empowered with
this dynamic content, users have taken control of which
applications work, when and how.

All of the traditional powerhouses have lost control of
content consumption, and increasingly its generation. The
traditional technology and media companies' jobs simply
remain to facilitate the optimal media experience for consumers and businesses alike. This means lots of bandwidth
for full access to any media form, anywhere, anytime. Users
increasingly demand diverse media usage across devices
(handsets, PDAs and laptops to T.V.s and PCs), and industries are scrambling to enable it.

To meet the anything, anytime, anywhere future, all
parts of the media and technology industries need dramatic increases in the amount of bandwidth available to
drive consumption (minimum targets of 1 GB by 2010,
according to Verizon CEO Ivan Seidenberg)[39]. The avail-

ability of this bandwidth in diverse mobile geographies, increased functionality and openness of content devices, and finally open application environments and standards allow further social media innovation to occur—and prosper. In 2010, it is anticipated that 20 users in one night will download and upload more content on the Internet than the entire country did in 1995. So what does that mean for marketers? For one thing, the "participation is marketing" principles outlined in this book will accelerate dramatically with increased bandwidth, functionality and applications.

The realities of today's environment is that 50 percent broadband penetration at 500kbps to 2 Mbps has barely made user-generated video the new hot application for Americans. Imagine what four more years of technological and social media application development combined with a 5,000 percent increase in bandwidth will do. Not just at the home, but on ubiquitous wireless networks throughout the world.

Discerning the specific future of social media usage in this kind of environment can be extremely frustrating for the best technology minds, much less for marketing executives and non-industry specific CxOS and entrepreneurs. However, there are some trends that are shaping up between the tea leaves, which we will leave you with.

In an interview for this book, Telecom visionary Jeff Pulver, who owns Pulver Media and writes the fantastic Pulver Blog, pointed out that both Japan and Europe are far ahead of North America with their technology infrastructure.[41] Using this as a guiding point, here are the technologies that I see having the greatest impact on social media.

Wireless

The Japanese and European environments are vastly superior in their mobile and wireless usages with portable content as a dramatic new player in the media environment. Drivers for the mobile market include affordable flat fees, and the ability to use new Web/mobile 2.0 services on their phones, such as podcasting, RSS feeds, and more user-generated content to utilize. These services vary, from mobile blogging platforms like Twitter and RSS feeds, to music downloads and video. Then there are increasingly intelligent devices, like the iPhone, hitting the market that will drive further units.[42]

AT&T has banked its future on this trend, declaring itself to be a wireless company at NXTComm. Randall Stephenson said that customers were calling the shots, that the company's job was now to build out broadband mobility to enable the ability for consumers and businesses to use any device for any reason. A core beginning for AT&T will be its exclusive distribution of the iPhone, an end-user device that provides a hybridization of several content trends, from video and music downloads, to traditional voice functions and e-mail. Stephenson believes the iPhone's a game changer, not only for the company, but also for the entire industry, unleashing the full power of mobile broadband.[43]

This predicted movement has started to happen. According to the Pew Internet Project, approximately one third of all adult American Internet users (34 percent) have logged onto the Internet by wireless means using a laptop, PDA or cell phone. These users are younger than traditional Internet users: 37 percent of the 18-34 group, while only 18 percent of the 35 to 49 group use wireless. Most telling yet, the Pew Internet study shows that wireless users have a different behavior set than land line users, tending to be much more connected, more frequently with different surfing patterns.[44] Clearly, the mobile trend offers the greatest possible impact on social media, and therefore marketers.

Video

Jeff Pulver indicated the United States was leading the world was in broadband IPT.V. usage.[45] Similarly, Motorola CEO Ed Zander said user-generated content is fueling everything and video was the primary area of growth.[46] The statistics back this dynamic trend, a result of broadband usage enabling vast amounts of video to be downloaded expeditiously over telecom networks. According to a survey conducted by Frank N. Magid Associates in 2006, 9 percent of 12 to 64-year-old Americans who used the Internet reported using online video daily. By the end of the first quarter in 2007, this number had risen to 14 percent of Americans 12 to 64 years old.[47]

In anticipation of this trend, handset, PDA and portable PC companies like Apple, HP Motorola and Samsung are incorporating video into many of their next generation devices. Enabling video and content distribution that leverages mobile access to broadband will be critical to future growth. The most popular content viewing devices in the world are easily cell phones (2.5 billion), T.V.s and only then PCs, said Zander during his NXTcomm keynote.[48]

Video on demand—from traditional programming to user-generated—represents a huge growth area for marketing. Leveraging video media will require new ways and approaches to marketing. Creating value for audiences will be a must. The static 30 second commercial of days gone by will not work.

Geographic Based Services

The final key area for growth will likely be geographic based services, specifically local search and location-based services. With the FCC mandating location based services be available in all cell phones, many equipment manufacturers are racing to install GPS chips into every cell phone.[49] The result is a $2.1 billion cottage industry in the United States. Industry pundits believe in extending mobile services and will drive the uptake of new services that deliver enhanced value to subscribers. From workforce management to navigation and location searches, the location based opportunity has great social media potential for application developers.[50]

As for marketers, the opportunity to provide real valuable information about their offerings to customers in their own real-time location is invaluable. Getting to the street level represents a huge opportunity. "Local search campaigns are often the most affordable and will bring traffic from your immediate market area," said Kim T. Gordan, Marketing Coach at *Entrepreneur Magazine*.[51]

One aspect of local search remains, push pin mash-ups showing locations of stores, homes and other information on satellite maps. These maps are quickly evolving to convey much more complex information on amp, including actual street images. Along with this dynamically evolving trend, market-leader Google Earth has already started to offer marketers advanced advertising.[52] Local search—at home or mobile—offers incredible potential because of its ability to get down to an individual community member's specific needs, wants and most importantly, exactly where they are at that time. It's at the heart of community, and offers the greatest potential for building value.

All three technologies—wireless, video and location-based services—are actively growing in dynamic function. Social media networks and content providers, including established players like YouTube, Twitter, Digg, FaceBook, and Google Earth are .already trying to leverage these technologies for user-generated purposes. Marketers need to monitor these technological developments closely as they continue to impact social media...and therefore marketing.

Parting Thoughts

The future impact of social media on marketing will be felt throughout all disciplines. When there are vast changes in the way people communicate, like social media, marketing tactics and entire programs need to be rethought. For some more consumer-based industries, a shift in marketing means an even more dramatic organizational change.

Participation Affects All Marketing

Fewer and fewer companies are able to retain the public's trust as faith shifts to the peer space. Today's customers expect to be listened to and understood. By being involved in social networks, a company can be in tune with what their customers' wants and needs are, and can apply what they've heard to their traditional and new media marketing programs. All marketing approaches will change, becoming oriented towards what the community wants, and using the preferred communication mechanisms of that community.

Impact on Public Relations

PR will need to execute campaigns that mean something to communities of buyers and users, instead of the current short sighted focus on getting media coverage. Along the same lines, spin is not a welcome element when pursuing bloggers. PR practitioners must be willing to reach out to their community and give them true, unfiltered participation or they will be doing their company a disservice in the social media realm. Adjustment in outreach tactics for PR professionals is imperative.

Impact on Advertising

Social media's effects on advertising can already be felt. Many television ads have been user-generated, companies offer games or cell phone content to their consumers, some even have corporate accounts on networks like Second Life. While some campaigns have failed, many have been successful at engaging potential consumers with their social media brand efforts. The key to low-resistance in new media advertising is contributing value to the community.

Impact on Other Marketing Forms

With social media continually evolving, a variety of groups will be determining what tactics are best utilized. Environment, users, brand experts and consultants, companies and agencies will collectively collaborate to forge great marketing. While PR and advertising are the aspects of marketing most affected by social media, others like direct mail and database marketing will see the one-on-one customer relationship take on much more importance.

Technology's Social Media Future

The constant evolution of content has yielded an environment where users want access seemingly anywhere at all times, and companies are making it their mission to facilitate that wish. In this way, the "participation is marketing" principles outlined in this book will accelerate dramatically with increased bandwidth, functionality and applications. The three applications of social media with the potentials for the largest growth are wireless Internet, video, and geographic based services. All three increase the users' ability to connect and communicate wherever, whenever, and with whomever they wish.

Notes

[1] Brian Solis, "The Future of Communications," PR 2.0, June 11, 2007 (http://www.briansolis.com/2007/06/future-of-communications-manifesto-for.html).

[2] Kipp Monroe, original interview, June 14, 2007.

[3] Gartner Group, "Gartner Says Consumerization of IT is a Major Threat to Enterprise Security," Media Newswire, June 14, 2007 (http://media-newswire.com/release_1052431.html).

[4] Aaron Reed, "IT Executives Cite Social Media as Most Trusted Source When Making Purchasing Decisions," SYS-CON Media, June 7, 2007 (http://www.sys-con.com/read/386254.htm).

[5] Ed Cotton "Every Company is Now a Media Company," influx, June 14, 2007 (http://www.influxinsights.com/blog/article/1416/every-company-is-now-a-media-company.html).

[6] Shel Holtz, original interview, June 11, 2007.

[7] Monroe, ibid.

[8] Scott Baradell, original interview, June 15, 2007.

[9] Todd Andrlik is widely credited for creating the power-ranking format. His Power 150 ranking of marketing blogs is a tremendous resource you can visit at: http://www.toddand.com/power150/.

[10] Ibid.

[11] Kami Watson Huyse original interview, June 11, 2007.

[12] Toby Bloomberg, original interview, June 9, 2007.

[13] August Busch IV, "2006 Letter to Shareholders," February 1, 2007 (http://www.anheuser-busch.com_pdf 2006AR_LetterToShareholders.pdf).

[14] Kami Watson Huyse, "Anatomy of a Social Media Campaign: Journey to Atlantis," Communication Overtones," May 3, 2007 (http://overtonecomm.blogspot.com/2007/05/anatomy-of-social-media-campaign.html).

[15] Ibid.

[16] Rob La Gesse, "Journey to Atlantis Debut: A blogger's perspective," Stuffleufagus, May 11, 2007 (http://lagesse.org/index.php/2007/05/11/journey-to-atlantis-debut-sea-world-san-antonio-a-bloggers-perspective/).

[17] Kami Watson Huyse, "PPT Case Study: SeaWorld San Antonio. Measuring Social Media Campaigns."

[18] David Meerman Scott, New Rules of Marketing & PR, p. 28.

[19] Ed. Victoria Neufeldt, Webster's New World College Dictionary, p. 1087.

[20] Kami Watson Huyse, original interview, June 11, 2007.

[21] Jeremy Pepper, "The Social Media Explosion via Dan Sheinman," Pop! PR Jots, June 5, 2007 (http://pop-pr.blogspot.com/2007/06/social-media-explosion-via-dan.html).

[22] David Meerman Scott, New Rules of Marketing & PR, p. 14.

[23] "The Nikon Blogger Outreach Program and Me," Tell Ten Friends, June 8, 2007 (http://www.telltenfriends.com/blog/2007/06/08/the-nikon-blogger-outreach-program-and-me/).

[24] Shel Holtz, original interview, June 11, 2007.

[25] Eric Eggertson, "The New PR Tools Gain Credibility, Lose Their Fad Status," Common Sense PR, June 23, 2007, (http://www.commonsensepr.com/2007/06/23/the-new-pr-tools-gain-credibility-lose-their-fad-status/).

[26] Geoff Livingston, "Advertising NEXT," TIA Telecommunities (http://blog.tiaonline.org/2007/06/20/advertising-next/) June 20, 2007.

[27] Craig Endicott and Kenneth Wylie, Ad Age Agency Report 2006, "Advertising Age," April 30, 2006 (http://adage.com/article?article_id=108906).

[28] Tim Leberecht, "No One is Watching Bud.T.V.," iPlot, (http://iplot.typepad.com/iplot/2007/05/no_one_is_watch.html).

[29] Richard Stacey, "10 Predicitions to Help Shape the Social Media Revolution," Social Computing Magazine, May 22, 2007.

[30] Shel Holtz, original interview.

[31] Kipp Monroe, original interview.

[32] Geoff Livingston, "Advertising NEXT."

[33] Valeria Maltoni, "What is Open Source Marketing," The Blog Herald, June 15, 2007 (http://www.blogherald.com/2007/06/15/what-is-open-source-marketing/).

[34] Valeria Maltoni, "Are You Ready for Marketing 2.0?," Conversation Agent, June 15, 2007 (http://www.conversationagent.com/2007/06/are_you_ready_f.html).

[35] Joe Lichtenberg," Brand Marketers, Meet Social Networks,"MarketingProfs.com, March 6, 2007.

[36] Solis, "The Future of Communications."

[38] Pike & Fischer, "U.S. Broadband Pentration to Hit 60% in 2007," January 6, 2007 (http://www.pf.com/getPdf.asp?id=451&type=PRESS).

[39] Geoff Livingston, "Verizon CEO and Chairman Ivan Seidenberg Keynote."

[40] Geoff Livingston, "And John Chambers," TIA Telecommunities, June 19 (http://blog.tiaonline.org/2007/06/19/and-john-chambers).

[41] Original interview with Jeff Pulver, June 18, 2007. You can visit Jeff's blog at: http://pulverblog.pulver.com/

[42] Richard McManus, "2007 WebPredictions," Read/Write Web, December 19, 2006 (http://www.readwriteweb.com/archives/2007_web_predictions.php).

[43] Geoff Livingston, "AT&T Randall Stephenson Keynote from NXTcomm," TIA Telecommunities, June 19, 2007, (http://blog.tiaonline.org/2007/06/19/att-randall-stephenson-keynote-from-nxtcomm/).

[44] John Horrigan, "Wireless Internet Access," Pew/Internet, February 2007 (http://www.pewinternet.org/pdfs/PIP_Wireless.Use.pdf).

[45] Jeff Pulver.

[46] Geoff Livingston, "Motorola Chairman & CEO Ed Zander Keynote," TIA Telecommunities, July 20 (http://blog.tiaonline.org/2007/06/20/motorola-chairman-ceo-ed-zander-keynote/).

[47] Frank N. Magid Associates, "Huge Growth Occurs in Online Video Usage," EarthTimes.org, June 18, 2007 (http://www.earthtimes.org/articles/show/news_press_release,124305.shtml).

[48] Geoff Livingston, "Motorola."

[49] Janice Partyka, "AGPS Makes It Happen," GPS World, April 18, 2007 (http://uc.gpsworld.com/gpsuc/article/articleDetail.jsp?id=420715).

[50] Chris Polito, "Location-based services version 2.0," Total Telecom, March 29, 2007 (http://www.totaltele.com/ View.aspx?ID=91162&t=4).

[51] Kim T. Gordan, "10 Marketing Trends to Watch in 2007," Entrepreneur.com, November 10, 2006 (http:// www.entrepreneur.com/marketing/ marketingcolumnistkimtgordon/article170208.html).

[52] Kristina Knight, "Google sending local ads to 'Earth,'" Biz Report, February 7, 2007 (http://www.bizreport.com/2007/02/ google_sending_local_ads_to_earth.html)

Chapter 6
Think Liquid

Regardless of technological change, the future of social media will be dictated by the community's rapid adoption of new media forms. Change occurs dynamically in online communities as new applications develop. Though behavior has changed, relationships must be maintained. That means marketers must be flexible while moving forward.

Hot social media networks and new technologies are constantly emerging. Whether it's Facebook or Mahalo or another social network du jour, marketers will continue to be faced with the consistent challenge of finding new ways to use media forms to engage the community. Like water, the marketer must move with the community, learning the newest technology's impact on communications. And like water, this type of activity follows the path of least resistance.

It's important to note that as "webolution" continues, marketers should avoid getting bedazzled by hot media forms. We've seen them come and go. Excite, Prodigy, AOL, Friendster, MySpace (fading, but still relevant), and increasingly Yahoo! are brands of the past. The passing of these demonstrates that professionally we cannot get too focused on specific technologies. Why? Because they will evolve, change, and in some cases, disappear.

Thinking Liquid in a Dynamic Environment

Marketers are better served by liquid fluidity in their thought processes and approaches. That way they can adapt to sudden changes and new, hot technologies as social media continues its march forward. As this natural process unfolds over time and communities evolve, their information needs and consumption of media will evolve, too.[1]

With increasingly diverse and changing marketing environments, successful marketers will focus on social media principles rather than tactics. Basic social media principles can serve as guidance no matter the environment. By relying on principles and using fluid approaches to meet the media form, marketers can best serve their communities of interest over time. Those who can't or won't play by the principles of social media risk irrelevance because they will not be able to adapt to change.

These principles have been well discussed throughout this book. Collectively, they are the basic rules for successful social media marketing and PR. One thing that is clear is that marketing communications and PR are about building relationships with the community as a whole and individual members. You can't command and control.

The Seven Principles
of Social Media Communications

1) Relinquish message control: Our first gut check in chapter two discussed the need to stop controlling the message. Social media experts have been touting this for years now. Though it is clearly necessary in social media realms, businesses are still struggling with relinquishing control.

Yet examined in the context of a relationship—which is the core of traditional PR as well as social media marketing—we see that two-way communications are at the heart of any relationship. Controlled relationships are considered dysfunctional on an individual basis and authoritative within a large community. Since social media is inherently two-way, a controlling entity that enters the community will be met with anger, distrust, and either rebellion or deaf ears by key stakeholders.

2) Honesty, ethics, and transparencies are musts: How can you have a relationship with one person or many if you don't behave well? This isn't about baring trade secrets or intellectual property. It's about basic human relations and creating a strong foundation for long-term, two-way, mutually beneficial relationships. Operate by the golden rule: Treating others as you'd want to be treated.[2]

3) Participation within the community is marketing: Just creating content is not enough. That's still a one-way mindset.

Get into the customer's realm. Comment and contribute to larger community groups and social networks. Read customer and related blogs (or vlogs and podcasts), and interact with the writers.[3] In short, your organization cannot gain the community's respect unless it is actually part of the community. Direct2Dell and its other social media forms are great examples. Dell not only hosts blogs and community sites, but actively engages on the community's own turf.

4) Communication with audiences is an outdated, 20th century concept: An audience is a 20th century mass communications concept. Audiences receive one-way communications—movies, radio broadcasts, speeches, etc. Thanks to social media, the audience members can now talk back, forcing organizations to address them in a conversational, two-way manner. Audiences are part of the command and control era, and social media marketing is community-based. The long-term results should become self-evident as discussions become much more active.[4]

5) Build value for the community: This is a strategic principle. When you are looking to "market," know your community. It is only by listening, reading, and understanding that community that you can serve it with valuable information. Building value for a group of people means making a core decision to create content for them regardless of the technology or social network.[5]

6) Inspire your community with real, exciting information: Your stakeholders have problems. Creating content for them does not mean giving them a press release. It means fighting for their interest, and delivering great content that speaks to them and helps resolve their concerns. Don't waste their time with product details. Instead, remember that the company's professional endeavors provide subject matter expertise that can be used to build intrinsic value.[6]

7) Intelligently manage the media form to build a stronger, more loyal community: Intelligently creating content to build a community also means making it easy for community members to come back. Create calls to action, use a central landing point like a blog or a corporate social media portal, and manage your RSS feeds intelligently; make your content locations obvious and accessible. And don't let your efforts become fallow. Cultivate sustained reader interest by creating and posting new content on a regular schedule.

Measuring the Results

These seven principles enable intelligent conversational marketing within a wide variety of social media forms. Though much of the social media marketing discussion revolves around the importance of engaging in a conversation, the participation marketing ethos, we all know that businesses blog and create social media campaigns to market themselves and make money.

Many companies discover that the results that they are looking for are the natural by-product of engaging with communities on their terms. In essence, a corporation or organization will be rewarded for being a good community member. [7]

We've already talked about Southwest Airlines' fantastic blog. As *Now Is Gone* moves to print, the airline has just revealed that it has garnered $150 million in ticket sales from its widget, part of its social media mix.[8]

Livingston Communications client Goodwill of Greater Washington loves its blog, its social media—engaged fashion show, and the dialogue it now engages in with the vintage industry. It also appreciates the more than 700 unique visitors the three-month-old blog receives weekly and its shopper conversion rate of 4.5%.

As these examples show, the discussion about corporate social media needs to include more than just ethics and conversation methods. In many ways, these principles represent the rules of engagement and forms of interaction, respectively. But most organizations need more.

At the end of the day, companies care about measurement. Businesses will demand results that are planned for byproducts of a conversation. This is the great challenge for marketing departments and social media consultants: Finding ways to build social media campaigns that deliver planned-for, measurable results. Measurement types can vary greatly, and results can include search engine optimization (SEO), impressions, transactions, changes in brand perception, and PR opportunities. Marketers must create a campaign that not only engages users, but also effectively reports progress.[9]

Parting Thoughts

Social media will continue to change as technologies advance. Marketers need to remain fluid in their approach towards conversations with the community. Readiness to adapt to new media forms and reliance on social media principles will enable marketers to succeed in their endeavors.

The Seven Social Media Principles

1. *Relinquish message control*
2. *Honesty, ethics, and transparencies are musts*
3. *Participation within the community is marketing*
4. *Communication to audiences is an outdated, 20th century concept*
5. *Build value for the community*
6. *Inspire your community with real, exciting information*
7. *Intelligently manage the media form to build a stronger, more loyal community*

Measuring the Results

Ultimately, conversation marketing in social media needs to produce results. You can achieve the results you want by engaging communities on their own terms with principle-based approaches. Remember: Corporations and organizations will be rewarded for being good members of the community. And if those rewards are measurable, so much the better.

Notes

[1] Kyle Flaherty, "My Six Truths on Social Media,"Engage in Pr, July 12, 2007 (http://www.engageinpr.com?p=254).

[2] Cam Beck, "10 Steps to a More Fulfilling Experience in the Show Room,"Chaos Scenario, August 10, 2007 (http://www.chaosscenario.com/main/2007/08/10-steps-to-a-e.html).

[3] Heuer.

[4] Rosen.

[5] Lewis Green, "Writing for and to Readers,"bizsolutionsplus, September 17, 2007 (http:/lgbusinesssolutions.typepad.com/ solutions_to_grow_your_bu/2007/09/writing-for-and.html).

[6] Steve Spalding, "How to Build a Start-Up,"How to Split an Atom, August 31, 2007 (http://howtosplitanatom.com/news/how-to-build-a-startup/).

[7] Chris Brogan, "The Myth of Evil in Social Media," Chris Brogan, September 17, 2007 (http://chrisbrogan.com/the-myth-of-evil-corporations-in-social-media/).

[8] Joan Voight, "Southwest Keeps Fans from Straying,"Ad Week, August 20, 2007 (http://www.adweek.com/awiq_interactive/article_display.jsp?vnu_content_id=1003627839).

[9] Kami Huyse, "Blog Traffic: List of Online Tools to Help Measure Who Is Coming to the Party" Communication Over-tones, September 18, 2007 (http://overtonecomm.blogspot.com/2007/09/blog-traffic-list-of-onlinetools-to.html).

Best of the
Buzz Bin Interviews

B eginning in early March, 2007, the Buzz Bin Blog
started featuring some of the industry's leading marketing minds and their thoughts on social media trends.
In many ways, the first interviews created the genesis for
this book, and later they became primary research vehicles.
Here are the best of the Buzz Bin interviews from March
through June, 2007 (in the spirit of blogging, they are
published in reverse chronological order):

Shel Holtz (June 19-21)
Toby Bloomberg (June 14)
Todd Defren (May 17)
Brian Oberkirch (May 1)
Laura Ries (April 23)
Kami Watse Huyse (April 20)
Scott Baradell (March 9)

Shel Holtz Discusses Social Media's Impact on Social Marketing

June 19-21, 2007

I usually like to write an introduction for our interviewees. Shel Holtz doesn't need one. We're honored to have him on the Bin. Without further ado, our interview with Shel Holtz.

BB: Tell us about your book and what it is going to do for marketers and everyone on the Internet.

SH: It's being published by McGraw-Hill and is part of their *How to Do Everything* series and it's called *How to Do Everything with Podcasting.* I co-authored it with Neville Hobson, who's the co-host of the twice-weekly podcast that I do called, *For Immediate Release,* which is actually a series of podcasts Neville and I do.

Twice a week, we produce *The Hobson and Holtz Report,* the cornerstone of *For Immediate Release,* which is a look at public relations as it's affected by social media and online communications. (*For Immediate Release* also includes interviews, book reviews, and recordings of speeches and panel discussions.) Neville and I were approached, and for about a year we have been working on this book that is just as the title says, how to do everything with podcasting. It's a little longer than most of the podcasting books you'll see because we cover things like how to use a podcast as a business tool or employee communications tool or marketing tool in addition to all the technical information that's included; really podcasting A to Z.

It's going on sale on the 15th, and should be available just about everywhere. In fact, last time I was at a Barnes and Noble I saw a whole rack of *How to Do Everything* books in their computer section, so I'm looking forward to seeing it there, as well as all the usual places, like Amazon.com and Barnesand Noble.com.

BB: *Where do you think social media is taking marketing in general? We all know it is the latest trend within marketing, but how is it affecting the marketing discipline as a whole?*

SH: I think it is affecting it greatly and it will continue to. I resist the notion that you have to put all your eggs in this basket because there still are a lot of people that are not engaging in social media. But, depending on the kind of market you're in, and in a lot of respects, regardless of the market you're in, people ignore it at their peril.

What's changing is the idea of who is in control of the message. Most marketers, for a long time, have had the luxury of delivering a message one way, top down, and they knew that people were going to listen and some were going to be influenced by what they saw or what they heard. There weren't a lot of ways you could go about vetting information that was offered to you.

For example, if you look at a typical T.V. commercial for a new car it will show the vehicle driving sideways in an inch of water throwing up this beautiful spray that the light is catching just right and at the end of the commercial you get about one-tenth of a second of very small type, and a lot of it. People would say, "Wow. I want that car. That's glorious. I want my car to look like that when I'm driving down the street." But you didn't know, until you got a TiVo, that if you freeze frame that legal type at the end, you can't make your car look like this.

It's done on a closed track with professional drivers wearing 5-point harnesses and parts of the car had been removed to make room for other things, and the disclaimer informs you that you shouldn't try this on the street. Marketing, in a lot of regards, was slick presentations that were designed to pull the wool over the consumers' eyes.

Today you *can* freeze frame with TiVo so you can see exactly what that legal disclaimer says. You can then capture it and put it up on the Web for everyone to see and people can talk about it to each other. This is what social media is all about; people talking to each other. We have seen fewer and fewer organizations able to continue to hold the public's trust as faith shifts to the peer space.

The reason the trust is shifting is because the original sources of information, business, mainstream media, and government have egregiously violated that trust on a number of occasions in the past several years. People trust people like themselves; they are able to reach out to those kinds of people with greater ease and with a larger pool thanks to social media.

Whether that's a blog, or a social network, or a wiki, if there's someone like you who says "I saw this movie. It sucked." Or "I have this car and you don't want the maintenance troubles I've had. Don't buy this car." That's where you are going to look for the information to help you make a decision, as opposed to being influenced by the slick T.V. commercials or the traditional one way, top down marketing. That doesn't mean there's no room for commercials or traditional marketing, but I think it does mean that it has to be balanced and integrated with social media involvement.

BB: Will consumers and buyers be less tolerant of traditional media tactics, and will traditional tactics have to evolve to incorporate the same tone? In essence, will an ad-campaign have to possess social media aspects and be conversational in tone?

SH: I think there's going to have to be some sort of a social media dimension to a lot of the advertising that goes on out there and you're starting to see some of this. T.V. commercials now invite you to submit content, or go to a site where you are going to find a greater level of interactivity or involvement with the audience, or what Jay Rosen calls "the people formally known as the audience."

So in essence, I definitely think that is the case. It will always depend on the nature of the advertisement. If I thought about it, I could probably pull out an advertiser or commercial where that kind of interaction isn't needed. But by and large, I think organizations are going to have to stop and think about the fact that any commercial you broadcast can be copied, uploaded to YouTube, and commented on.

In addition, people are going to make their own commercials. This has been happening over the last couple of weeks with Apple's iPhone. The writer of the Brand New Day Blog for *BusinessWeek* said that he saw this commercial and he thought it was from the advertising agency for the iPhone, but then somebody e-mailed him and said "No, no.

This is just a fan who made this commercial." There is this consumer generated content, and companies are smart enough to figure out that you can get your fans to create this stuff for you.

Southwest Airlines, for example, is one of the companies that has had a contest inviting people to submit video. They had to be 20-seconds in length, and oriented to be one of those "Want to get away?" commercials. The winning ad would be produced as a national advertising spot. The videos could be uploaded and commented on, and the winning entry, which is pretty funny and very well produced, is going to be one of their regular national spots. They started with social media on the front end and it ended up being a regular, old T.V. commercial.

It doesn't matter which way you go, as long as you are out there engaging in that conversation on some level.

BB: So you really see a participation-as-marketing approach, where building community value comes first, than in the traditional forms?

SH: Absolutely. People don't understand this, but I talk about brand, and people think you are talking about a trademark or a logo, but the brand itself is the way the consumer reacts when they hear your company name or see your logo or a product of yours on store shelves. That is all based on their experience and the one way, top down, pushed advertising and marketing is only part of that ex-perience.

What always amazes me is how companies spend so much time on how to cut costs in their call centers and customer service, yet the experience you have with a call center or customer service is going to shape a person's perception of that brand tremendously. One reason I've always thought the call center needs to report to PR or communications and not wherever it reports now is because you want to invest in that and make that portion of your business absolutely rock so the experience people have is one where their experience was great and then they tell other people about how that experience was.

You can shape that perception of the brand through engagement in the conversation. For example, I have a blog that is dedicated to my business travel and I only really use it when I'm angry. I'm probably going to be spending half the year on the road and I experience a lot in hotels and airports with airlines and skycaps and the like. I had a bad experience with an off-airport parking service that I use and I blogged it.

The first comment that was posted was by an administrator with that company and she was saying, "We really try to be a better company than that. I'm really sorry that you had this experience and I'd like to make it right. Can I send you some free parking? If you send me the name of the driver, we'll deal with that."

That is what I tell people about, not the fact that I spent an hour waiting at the curb at 1 in the morning, which was my original gripe. All I talk about now is, and pardon me for using the "e" word, but they empowered a front office employee who stumbled upon my post to take action about it. I didn't get the usual corporate drivel from marketing services or whichever department would normally respond to something like that, if anybody responds at all.

I got a real, live human being reaching out to me and saying "We'll fix this." That's terrific. That's what organizations are going to have to start doing.

BB: How do you see the new trend impacting individual disciplines, such as public relations, as a profession?

SH: It's already affecting public relations as a profession. If you recognize that people are being influenced by their peers, and more and more of their peers are communicating online, not necessarily on a blog, but a conversation over networks like MySpace. If you look where younger folks, ages 14 to 26, are communicating, it's on MySpace.

It's not with a formal blog where you are trying to wield influence; it's just a conversation with your friends. Nevertheless, that's where influence is taking place. It becomes necessary to engage in some outreach with people you are able to determine are influential; that means reaching out to bloggers, podcasters, or just people who have heavily trafficked social-network profiles. It's not like reaching out to media, which is crafting a press release and making sure that your wire service hits the right markets. You have to reach out individually.

That's a whole different ballgame and there are PR agencies, even the world's largest in Fleishman-Hillard, looking for social media consultants. The agencies are starting to recognize, and some of them have recognized it earlier, that influence isn't all through the media anymore; with growing regularity its taking place in the social media space. I think you're also going to see a more rapid uptake of the social media news release-type framework.

There has been some resistance to this idea, but I think some people don't understand that it's not the news release that's social; it's the content that you want to get into the hands of bloggers, podcasters and people who write in online journalism venues. You're looking to provide the content to them in a format that they would want to use, where they don't have to struggle with it and sort of hammer it into the social media context that they want to put it in. Hewlett-Packard recently put out a social media news release and I thought that was remarkable.

BB: How do you see social media impacting the way brand managers do their job?

SH: I guess that depends on what a particular brand manager does within an organization. But I think people who are responsible for the brand are going to have to be aware about what is already being said about them out there in that space. In a lot of ways, this is really traditional communications.

You identify where the pockets of conversation are going on, and then you can classify that communication as positive, neutral, or negative. This is just good, old-fashioned, content analysis. Then you have to figure out what you are going to do about it in terms of the existing perceptions of the brand.

You also have to address any new initiatives that you have; new product launches or campaigns. Through the initial research that you have done, you'll know who is likely to talk about that, and do it in a way that doesn't make some people inclined to change the conversation as to how clueless you were in the approach you took to reaching out to the social media.

Right now, for example, there is a lot of chatter going on in the blogosphere about Nikon giving a whole bunch of bloggers cameras and how that was simply blogger bribery. I guarantee you that's not the conversation Nikon wanted.

BB: A lot of what is happening can be very intimidating to a company looking at social media, seeing all this volatility. What would you tell a company that knows it has to get involved in social media, but sees this and doesn't really have an idea as to how to approach it?

SH: I would counsel these organizations not to be taken in by a lot of the negativity they are going to read about in the media. The media thrives on uncertainty and doubt so they tend to report on all the negative items. There is a tremendous advantage to be gained through effective use of social media. I would start by listening. I would suggest the company spends a fair amount of time listening to what's being said before jumping in.

If you are going to start commenting on blogs, read a lot of comments, notice what happens in the comment stream and how people react. If you are going to blog, look at the blogs of your competitors, or ones that have a reputation for getting it right.

Just spend a lot of time absorbing how the conversation works in general, especially in whatever corner of the blogosphere you are going to be operating in; I would say 90 days isn't an unreasonable amount of time to spend really just soaking it all in. It will make things just that much more natural figuring out how you are going to play in that space if you're up to speed on the conversation that is already out there.

BB: *How much of this is really social media, versus understanding who your community is and really getting to know them better?*

SH: I'm getting to the point where I believe social media is really just integrated with everything else. By getting to understand your community, you'll understand what realm of social media they are engaged in and what space outside of social media they are engaged in. If you are thinking about creating a positive brand experience, you are going to want any encounter they have with your brand to be positive.

Whether it's in-store with a customer service representative, or online, increasingly, the online space is being dominated by social media. It really is understanding your community. If your community isn't online, then you get to pay attention to this a whole lot less. In rural towns where 60 percent of the population or so doesn't have access to computers, if the mayor simply blogs about a new parking ordinance, a lot of people will be getting parking tickets.

A company needs to ask itself, if they decide their community is active in the social media environment and they wish to pursue a social media program, what topics should they should be chiming in on, who are the important people they need to reach, should they be initiating the conversation or jumping into existing ones, and who should be representing the company. All kinds of different answers will become evident if you know the audience that you are trying to reach.

Social Media Nouveaux Answers
from Toby Bloomberg

June 14, 2007

She was our first interview on the Buzz Bin. When it came time to do research for *Now Is Gone*, Toby Bloomberg was one of the few resources I reached out to for primary research. Her Diva Marketing Blog is always top ranked, and she is one of the kindest, most accessible bloggers out there.

BB: Suddenly, many corporate marketers are approaching social media as a new way to reach their target audiences. What do you think of this?

TB: I think it's a terrific idea. Companies who step into social media now will be perceived as innovators. The big benefit is they'll have a head start on the "learnings" which will leap frog them over their competitors.

BB: Why are so many businesses running towards new media?

TB: The "so many" at this point is a relative term. For those organizations (non-profit, for profit, government) that think they have missed the virtual boat, it is moving out of dry dock; there is no need for swimming yet, but it is quickly picking up speed.

As to why the interest, organizations are realizing that many of their customers are hanging out on blogs, in mashup communities, on video sites, and gaming sites. Just like in the traditional world of media, marketers want to have a presence where their customers are likely to be.

For marketers who are early adopters it's cool to be seen in 3-D worlds like Second Life. Smart business people understand that new media offers multiple benefits, from enhanced search engine optimization, to new tools to obtain customer feedback and additional value-added content. Social media really shines at creating relationships, which are the first steps to customer acquisition and the reinforcement of customer retention.

However, social media is more than a passive Web site strategy. The most beneficial aspect is the ability to engage directly with customers and other stakeholders. Social media opens the doors for businesses to listen to the unfiltered voices of their customers and to track those conversations. Social media also provides opportunities for the *people* within the company to join in on those conversations and talk directly to customers. Taking an active role in creating a dialogue with customers about issues that they care about, at the moment in time when they care about those concerns, is the heart of new media marketing.

BB: What do you think of the terminology "target audience" versus "community?"

TB: Very interesting question. It seems to me that although the concepts are not mutually exclusive, the ideas you present are part of a process. You would first identify your target audience and understand their needs. Next, would come community building as a strategy to fulfill those needs. Keep in mind that not all of your target audience will want to join your "community." To go beyond what has become a buzz word, building community takes continuous effort and resources, which reverts back to marketing planning and delivering against your brand promise.

BB: What will happen to marketers who try to exploit social networks?

TB: I'll respond with a typical marketer's answer, "It depends." It depends how you define "exploit" in terms of adding benefit to the network. A good example from the healthcare blogoshere is a closed social networking community of physicians. The free community allows only physicians who can be confirmed against a data base of certified doctors to can gain access.

However, it allows paid sponsors the privilege of actively participating in the conversations that take place within the guarded walls of the community. Would you call this exploitation of a social networking community? Some would, but the members must perceive value because the community is growing rapidly.

BB: What are your thoughts on the concept "participation is marketing?"

TB: I love the concept. It adds an important dimension to an expanding, complex marketing tool bag. Sometimes it's nice to reach for a paper sales sheet with just the facts. It's also nice to know that there is an online communication resource: a bulletin board, blog, wiki, vlog, or podcast, where additional information can be found, including peer-to-peer feedback and a way to engage with the people in the company too.

BB: *How about the latest trend of traditional press releases evolving towards a social media releases?*

TB: Since the technology is available to include mixed media, video, links, photos, etc, why not capitalize on providing robust information in one place? What tends to frustrate me is the written information is sometimes too brief. The format leaves it up to the recipient to piece the elements of the story together. Sometimes I don't have time or want to watch a video or listen to a podcast. Nor do I want to think too hard. I want the story to be told and then I'll take it and modify it for my readers.

I want it all. Available links, multimedia and the story pulled together, along with the facts separated out.

BB: *What's the best thing a business can do if it's considering entering the blogging or social media world?*

TB: Understanding the culture. Blogging/social media is unlike any other marketing strategy I've seen. Since it is built on a culture that incorporates community. As with any community, there are social norms that new comers must be aware of. Informal checks and balances are in place and if you color out side of the lines, the blogosphere is not shy about letting you know.

Frequently, that slap on the hand is not contained within the confines of a few blog posts, but is picked up by mainstream media. The impact to the goodwill of the brand or business may be significant. The most critical aspects to keep top of mind are: honesty, transparency, authenticity.

The next step, after understanding the culture, is to give social media the respect of any valid marketing strategy. Set goals and objectives that relate back to business outcomes. How to measure the success of a social media strategy may be different than those of traditional marketing, however to gain credibility, we cannot be afraid to overlay accountability on social media tactics.

Then build strategies that support the brand while maintaining the authenticity of the conversation.

PR Squared's Todd Defren Talks About Social Media Releases

May 17, 2007

Todd Defren has many titles: Father of the Social Media Release, Author of PR Squared, and of course, there is his day job, Principal at SHIFT Communications. Todd took time to chat with the Buzz Bin about new media and the current state of the social media release. One great quote: "If a marketer is bent on 'exploiting' anything, it will likely bite him in the ass. That was *always* the case, of course, but in the Social Media world, the difference is that you'll be caught out more quickly, and the 'punishment' can be more harsh and more long-lasting." Read on for more...

BB: Suddenly many corporate marketers are approaching social media as a new way to reach their target audiences. What do you think of this?

TD: I am in favor of marketers who are willing to experiment with this type of approach. I would only caution them to leave their own caution at the door: to engage, you must fully embrace the opportunity to interact directly with customers.

This can be great, and get great results—if the product/service is great, and the outreach and participation (of the marketer) is candid and responsive. But the community can also be harsh and quick to judge and feels no compunction to always get the facts straight. That's daunting to most marketers, as it should be, but I think that the plusses outweigh the challenges.

BB: What do you think of the terminology "target audience" versus "community?"

TD: I don't get worked up about such distinctions. Life is too short to engage in semantic arguments like this one.

BB: What will happen to marketers who try to exploit social networks?

TD: The easy answer is "You will reap what you sow." If a marketer is bent on "exploiting" anything, it will likely bite him in the ass. That was ALWAYS the case, of course, but in the Social Media world, the difference is that you'll be caught out more quickly, and the "punishment" can be more harsh and more long-lasting.

My advice is to start any Social Media campaign by listening and quietly participating (as a user, not a marketer): this is the best way to "find the line;" to get a true sense for community standards.

BB: What are your thoughts of the concept "participation is marketing?"

TD: I totally agree. Speaking as a consumer, when I notice that a company takes an active, helpful role in community interactions, I am impressed and more favorably inclined to their brand.

BB: As the original creator of the social media release, what do you think of the latest trend of traditional press release wire services evolving towards a social media release format?

TD: I think that this is a good and necessary trend.

BB: Why are social media releases better for the current media environment?

TD: The strength of the SMNR is its ability to democratize access to the content and multimedia with which we tell stories on the Web. Anyone can rip content from the SMNR and use it within their own publishing forum as they see fit. This serves to widely disseminate news, and also gives consumers and publishers more input on the evolution of the newsmaker's story and brand.

In addition, the SMNR creates more dialogue and context around each news item. Done right, the SMNR becomes a blog post, which lives on its own microsite, with moderated comments, trackbacks, etc. that show the interplay of the news with the news consumer.

BB: What has to happen for the social media release to become more widely adopted?

TD: Adoption by major brands as a standard vs. a test case. More case studies of success.

I think it will be a long haul, but ultimately all we are talking about is making the press release more interactive, "audiotastic" and "visualizzy." It's a way to disseminate and democratize news by taking advantage of Web technology and multimedia…I'm betting on the SMNR's eventual domination. Check out the Before and After (using the SHIFT template) at Belkin's Web site. Which release would you rather read? Case closed.

Insights That Matter from Brian Oberkirch

May 1, 2007

Brian Oberkirch says what he thinks on LikeItMatters, and it works. This maverick marketer has an air of success, and when you read his insights into the new media environment, you'll understand why. When talking about corporate social networking, he says, "If your group is not really into open communication, responsiveness, acknowledging the real things customers are talking about, then blogging or any other social media project probably won't seem that useful to you." Read on for more great insights from Brian.

BB: How did LikeItMatters become one of the higher ranked marketing blogs?

BO: Well, I'm not sure 1) that it's highly ranked or 2) that it's a marketing blog. It started off as a place for me to talk about relevance in marketing and also technologies

(Tivo, etc) that allowed for filtering and better information matching. Now I seem to write mostly about developing Web-based services, social media, and sometimes, unmarketing.

The way any blog becomes popular is simple: blog often, link a lot, and respond in a meaningful way to what people say. Repeat. Often. Good bloggers read a ton and go out of their way to point you to good stuff. If you think it's about standing on a soapbox telling the world what *you* think, that doesn't bode well.

BB: How has blogging benefited your business?

BO: It's basically created my business. Five years ago I was doing traditional PR and marketing for tech companies and all my business came from people I knew personally. Today, I work primarily on Web projects and the number of people I 'know' is exponentially larger. New work and new colleagues happen all the time because of blogging: either someone finds my site, or I find someone I really want to work with, and we start talking. Blogs are a great way to start talking to someone or to keep on talking with someone you meet at a conference or somewhere. It's like a running meeting that doesn't have to stop.

BB: Your blog comments a lot of the failures in business blogging, agreeing that all senior execs "need to walk the halls" before they engage in social media. What's the big disconnect in corporations?

BO: I don't know that there is a big disconnect in corporations, per se. We could look at great blogging coming out of Microsoft, Sun, Yahoo, Boeing, and so on. It's more important what sort of cultural expectations the social media project comes up against. The tools themselves aren't magic. If your group is not really into open communication, responsiveness, acknowledging the real things customers are talking about, then blogging or any other social media project probably won't seem that useful to you. In fact, it might feel threatening. So, it's less the size of the company and more the attitude you have. I'd also say that most companies are not really prepared for how much work these programs entail. Lots of homework. There aren't any shortcuts. Before jumping into anything, I'd ask: why are we doing this? Is it because blogging or social networking feels hot and therefore we 'have to get in on it'? Or, do we have real business objectives that can be more efficiently met by utilizing social media.

BB: There seems to be a big focus on emerging media forms like Twitter and Second Life right now. Which one of these do you really like and why?

BO: Personally, I'm a huge fan of Twitter, and I think they have a lot right when it comes to building a lightweight Web app that users and other developers can bend to their will. I've seen some 'how to market via Twitter' pieces here and there, and I think it's a little early for that. A bit of the bandwagon effect.

Instead of asking 'how can we use this tool to get our messages out', ask 'why is this resonating with a certain audience?' What is the need that this fulfills? Again, all this is more about the users than it is companies who want to use these as messaging platforms. That is probably the least interesting thing.

If you just took Twitter (and there are a few tools out there) as a live focus group, and listened to what people say publicly on the spur of the moment, you'd probably learn a lot. You'd see what makes them thrilled to pieces, and when. You'd see their frustrations with certain services and processes. You'd see how small groups of people influence larger groups. It's a great lab. But mainly, I use it to keep up with my friends. It makes me happy to know where everyone is and what they are up to. I like Plazes for the same reason.

BB: What tips would you offer other bloggers?

BO: Focus on building the tribe one person at a time. Forget the Technorati 100 thinking. Being famous to 15 people is a huge advantage if they are the right 15 people. Keep in mind that blogging mostly has indirect effects: that you are building an online resume for yourself that is going to reward you in ways you really can't predict. Honor your readers' time. Give them great stuff to think about. Link generously. Answer anything you can.

BB: Do you see social networking as an art or a science?

BO: I think it's a natural extension of the social interactions people have always had. We like to affiliate with likeminded people. The Web extends the type of connections that are possible, so geography impedes us less than it did. Word of mouth has always been powerful. As parents, we ask other parents how they do things, what suggestions they might have, how their kids react to certain things. Now we have the ability to tap more than just the people on our street, at work or in our PTA. The thing to understand from a marketing perspective is that now anyplace on the network can potentially feed a story to anywhere else on the network. Trends will accelerate faster. Flame out quicker. Bad news will certainly travel farther and faster and feel more real (e.g. a video of one laptop blowing up makes the battery crisis seem like something worth paying attention to). I think all the skills PR people and marketers have been cultivating are going to be really useful in this new world, but things happen much faster and response and iteration are probably more important than rendering pixel perfect creative work.

BB: *Last December's Time person of the year article really seemed to legitimize blogging and other Web 2.0 technologies. How did this impact the blogosphere?*

BO: Big events like elections and disasters have put blogs and DIY media in the spotlight. By 2005 it was certainly commonplace to have people talking about the business applications of these tools. There is no blogosphere as much as there are hundreds of thousands of little networks that revolve around certain topics. These tools work really well in micro communities. The more niche your offering, the better suited it probably is for social media.

I guess you can do Coke stuff in Second Life, which I saw today, but that seems to me to be beside the point.

As my friend John Moore says: Blogs help small businesses seem big and big businesses feel small. And that's a huge thing to be able to pull off. But it's not a magic bullet, and we should take a hard look at just what we're trying to accomplish with all this.

Origin of Brands Author Laura Ries Discusses New Media

April 23, 2007

Laura Ries is one of the most respected minds in marketing today. I remember seeing her speak as a guest of the Greater Washington Board of Trade, and promptly bought ten copies of her latest book to give to associates. Laura and father Al Ries' collective works have easily influenced ten million marketers, and her new blog, Origin of Brands, has quickly ascended to become one of the most well read destinations on the Internet.

With a new Ries via Internet video series about to be launched, Laura took some time to discuss new media's impact on brands. What better way to celebrate one year in business than publishing this thought provoking interview.

BB: How do you like blogging as compared to speaking and writing books?

LR: Writing a book is a long and sometimes agonizing process. A book can take years from the time you write the words down until the time someone reads them. Once written and published, however, a book can reach hundreds of thousands of people around the world in almost every language for many years. Al's book, *Positioning*, is still in print 26 years after it was first published. All of the four books we have written together are still in print. Speaking live in front of an audience is exhilarating because of the audience feedback. But speeches require a lot of planning, contracts and travel time. Even in business class, sitting on an airplane for 24 hours is not all it's cracked up to be. And one speech can only reach maybe 1,000 people at a time.

Writing a blog is the best of both worlds. You have the ability to reach a mass audience on a global scale immediately. It affords me the opportunity to comment on breaking business news and relate our branding laws to the situation. A blog can also reach people with a frequency not possible with either a book or speech. Making a trip to India certainly cannot be done on a weekly basis.

BB: Has communicating with the blogosphere via Origin of Brands benefited your business?

LR: I believe my blog has greatly benefited our business. Fans of our books and/or our speeches can sign up and get my latest blog post as well as read posts from the archive which offers a treasure trove of ideas, advice and observations.

Our consulting business also benefits. Having a blog keeps us current and relevant in the new Internet age. It also gives prospects a constantly updated catalog of our branding philosophy. Reading our books and/or blogs is what drives people to pick up the phone or e-mail us to book a consulting session.

BB: Your blog comments a lot on major brands and their strengths and weaknesses. Can you discuss how new media can positively affect a brand?

LR: Word of mouth is what builds brands today. But you still need a way to get that first mouth moving. The best way is by PR, not advertising. Advertising doesn't have the credibility to drive the word of mouth process. Also, PR benefits from the proliferating choices of new media outlets. Compared to decades ago, there are more places today to generate PR.

BB: And conversely, how can it negatively impact a brand?

LR: As quickly and as easily as PR can build a brand, PR can take a brand down. Negative PR is incredibly damaging. And with the growth of new media, mainly the Internet, it can happen faster than ever. Look no farther than Don Imus, JetBlue or Taco Bell for proof of this fact.

Luckily, we live in a celebrity obsessed society. This means that famous people and famous brands are always given a second chance. The ability for famous people and brands to generate PR gives them the tools they would need to rebuild what negative PR has destroyed.

Non-famous people or brands can be annihilated by even mild scandals. If you're not famous, you seldom get a second chance.

BB: How will new media impact the creation and diversification of brands as outlined in your book, the Origin of Brands?

LR: The Origin of Brands says that over time more and more brands will inhabit the earth. (It's an analogy with the book, *The Origin of Species*, which states that over time, more and more species will inhabit the earth.) The best way to succeed is by being first in a new category and then creating a brand to dominate that category, as Apple did with the iPod, the first high-capacity MP3 player.

You can also be successful today by creating categories that serve small market segments. The Internet gives brands the ability to reach even the most narrow of segments profitably.

Niche is no longer a dirty word in branding. A niche can become a billion dollar brand. Red Bull and Under Armour, for example.

BB: What are your favorite blogs?

LR: CK's Blog (http://www.ck-blog.com), Brand Autopsy (http://brandautopsy.typepad.com/brandautopsy/), and B.L Ochman's, What's Next Blog (http://www. whatsnextblog .com/).

BB: Last December's Time person of the year article really seemed to legitimize blogging and other Web 2.0 technologies. How did this impact the blogosphere?

LR: You answered your own question. The *Time* "Person of the Year" article gave blogging and Web sites credibility and legitimacy as an alternative source of information. Credibility is both the most difficult to attain and most valuable thing an industry needs to survive. Now that the blogosphere has it, it is sure to survive, evolve and diverge.

Kami Watse Huyse Communicates
Social Network Overtones

April 20, 2007

Kami Watson Huyse is one of the talented successful PR pros who has successfully navigated into the new media environment. Communication Overtones is one of my favorite reads, and given her ranking in the blogosphere, it's apparent I am not the only one. She discusses the plethora of new social networks, the fatigue they can cause, and their dynamic impact in news and crisis situations. Read on to learn more about Kami's views on social networks.

BB: How has Communication Overtones benefited your business?

KWH: It has served as an educational tool for both me and also for my clients. It serves as a place to get instant feedback on ideas and tactics that we might be considering for a client. It has also helped us find and develop new business.

BB: How can new media forms help during a crisis PR situation?

KWH: New media provides a means by which one can open a direct and instantaneous channel of communication with those who care most about an issue. Also, it is a no-fuss way to get information out fast. Look at the incident at Virginia Tech. Social media sites served as a way for people to quickly connect and also for reporters to get rich information quickly. I think organizations that don't factor new media into their crisis planning will pay the price in public sentiment

BB: What do you think are the biggest issues facing the new media industry?

KWH: I think one of the biggest is fatigue. In how many new platforms and communities can one person realistically join and participate fully? For companies, the question becomes, "Which of these networks are most important for us to participate within?" I think that organizations run the risk of running after the latest gizmo in order to keep up with the competition. This is still a business decision, the extent to which a company or organization wades into the social media waters still needs to be based on strategic principles.

BB: What are your favorite social networks and why?

KWH: Back to the last question, I am a member of way too many networks and may be bordering on overload. I regularly use YouTube, mostly for clients; Flickr, to add some spice to my blog; and del.icio.us to for bookmarking and also for monitoring for clients. These three, in addition to my blog, which at present is hosted at Blogger.com, are my workhorses.

I also am on Twitter, which is fun, but which is still peripheral, and I do a great deal in Second Life. Namely, I have monthly meetings of marketers and PR folk there in my Second Tuesday in Second Life series. Additionally, I have a Facebook and MySpace site, as well as a profile on LinkedIn.

BB: What corporate blogs/social networking initiatives do you admire and why?

KWH: I have admired Southwest Airlines entrance into the new media space. Their blog is fun, but at the same time addresses the pressing issues when necessary. I think they have done a fine job of balancing the informational needs of those that read the blog, and also of pulling in participation from across their employee base. The blog really affirms their existing culture, and I think it was sage of them to capitalize on that.

BB: What tips would you offer other corporate bloggers?

KWH: Be real, be open and be willing to let criticism ride. I think that the companies that allow the critical feedback to appear on their site are winning points with customers. Just last week I conducted a focus group and asked the participants what they felt inferred credibility to a Web site. They said many things, but one that stood out to me was that they felt unvarnished consumer feedback added credibility. The day of the filtered "testimonial" is dead. Most customers know that it is a bunch of hooey.

BB: Time magazine dubbed bloggers person of the year. What's next for our industry?

KWH: Actually they dubbed YOU, the person of the year— meaning that there must be recognition that ordinary people are now the content creators. Niche blogs that have a small but respectable audience are the gatekeepers of information about that topic. Certainly the mainstream media has recognized this and regularly uses bloggers as a source. But more important than that is if there is a vacuum of information, people will create their own.

Again, think of how word of mouth worked at Virginia Tech to get the news out about the shootings. We live in a world where this is happening, and we as communicators are obliged to understand it and use it for the better good of our organizations and the people they serve.

Media Orchard Creator Scott Baradell
Spins New Thicket

March 9, 2007

Idea Grove President, Scott Baradell, launched his company two years ago. As part of his marketing effort, he created the Media Orchard Blog, which soon became one of the most popular blogs on the Internet.

Now he's started, Spin Thicket, an online community for marketing, media, PR and advertising folks. As a big fan of Spin Thicket, I've asked Scott to be the next Diary Interview and share some of his thoughts with us. The results are excellent, providing some deep insights from this marketing pioneer.

BB: What made you start Spin Thicket when you already had a successful blog, Media Orchard?

SB: When I started Media Orchard in March 2005, I knew nothing about blogging. My first couple months of posts were pretty tentative; I was worried about offending potential clients so I was careful not to talk too much about politics, controversial topics, things like that. At some point, I started opening up and sharing who I was through the blog. It was a breath of fresh air for me, and I found the creative juices carried over to my client work.

But after 2,000 blog posts, I wanted to try something different. Spin Thicket is an attempt to build an online community, which I think most people would agree is a more difficult challenge than writing a blog. As with Media Orchard, I've centered Spin Thicket on the kind of content I enjoy—because as soon as it's not fun, it's not worth doing.

BB: *How have these sites benefited your business?*

SB: When I started Media Orchard I had *no* clients who were blogging or had any interest in blogs. Right now, I'm helping virtually *all* of my clients with blogs and/or online communities.

A lot of agencies and consultants present themselves as blogging experts but haven't done much to back it up. I reached the top 2,800 blogs on Technorati at Media Orchard's peak last year—and I think that communicates more to a client than some PowerPoint presentation on Web 2.0.

BB: *What's your favorite aspect of the new media environment?*

SB: I like a lot of things about it. I'm an information junkie. When I was growing up, I read the newspaper every single day—even when I was a little kid. Then I became a newspaper reporter. I love having all these sources of information to choose from. Highly addictive.

BB: *How has the new media (blogs, video, etc.) impacted the PR and marketing profession?*

SB: In so many ways—and we've only scratched the surface. There's been so much talk about corporate blogging and social media news releases that it's distracted corporate marketers from what will impact them the most—the underlying medium, rather than how it's currently used.

To provide just one small example, the Idea Grove has been doing a lot of television pitches recently for one of our clients. A couple years ago, we might have had the client shoot b-roll and distribute it via satellite—which isn't cheap. With this client, we've had great success simply sending an e-mail note with a link to the video on YouTube.

Everyone knows about YouTube. But there are new tools emerging all the time—and most of them (for now anyway) are free. What's a better deal than that?

BB: What tips would you offer other PR pros?

SB: The best way to learn is simply to get involved. Start a blog. Join a community. Comment on other people's blogs. Subscribe to a bunch of RSS feeds that you like, and make checking them part of your morning routine.

If you choose to start a blog, though, here's an idea: Write about something you enjoy! Don't become another generic PR blog, trying to impress prospective clients with posts, like "5 Ways to Get Bloggers to Write About Your Company," and "12 Things to Do When a Blogger Says Something Bad About Your Company," and "37 Ways to Scratch Yourself in Your Boxer Shorts While Writing a Blog Post."

Be yourself. People—and clients are people, too—like that.

BB: *Do you see social networking as an art or a science?*

SB: I'm not heavy user of social networks. I've started MySpace sites, YouTube accounts, MyBlogLog and so on, but I haven't followed through with them as I'd like to. It's just too time-consuming. But I'd say that social networking is part art and part science.

The same is true of blogs, by the way. Brian Clark over at Copyblogger has certainly turned it into a science. His topics, how well he promotes them, how quickly he adds subs—it's pretty amazing. He has a special talent.

I've always been a bit hit and miss—more artsy, I guess. For example, the most popular post I ever wrote was something called "The 10 Greatest Countries in the History of the World." It was completely off-topic for Media Orchard. Somehow, it's ended up getting 100,000 hits in two days.

It's kind of like the songwriter who spends months writing songs that go nowhere, and then scribbles something down on a napkin that becomes a huge hit.

BB: *Last December's Time person of the year article really seemed to legitimize blogging and other Web 2.0 technologies. What's next for the blogosphere?*

SB: Frankly, I think it's going to get ugly as corporations continue to exert their influence over it; the process has only just begun.

When you think about it, Web 2.0 started the way Web 1.0 started. That is, you had a bunch of techies and academics and anti-corporate types running everything and thinking they could make the rules for everybody else. But guess what? They can't. We live in a deregulated market economy—

and ultimately, where there is money to be made, the market will make the rules.

I'm not saying that this is a good thing or a bad thing; I'm just saying it's inevitable. It's inevitable in the same way that cable news stations will cover Anna Nicole Smith 24/7, no matter what's going on in Africa. All this social media stuff is going mainstream; it's all going to be owned and operated by companies that are trying to wring every dollar they can out of it.

So the geeks who think they rule the world right now are going to get a reality check from big business. The lucky few will get a cashier's check as well.

Blog Roll

The following bloggers had either blog posts cited in and/
or were interviewed for *Now Is Gone*. These sources are listed
permanently on the *Now Is Gone Blog* (*www.nowisgone.com*)
to honor them and provide business readers additional source
material. The book's sources are:

- Teli Adlam, *The OptiNiche Blog*
- Adam Aleman, *FlashReport*
- Todd Andrlik, *Todd And: The Power to Connect*
- Scott Baradell, *Media Orchard*
- Cam Beck, *Chaos Scenario*
- Richard Becker, *Copywrite*
- Jordan Behan, *Tell Ten Friends*
- Toby Bloomberg, *Diva Marketing Blog*
- Bob, *Bob Meets World*

- Kristina Bouweiri, *Make It Better*
- Chris Brogan, *Chris Brogan*
- C.C Chapman, *Reality Bitchslap*
- Ed Cotton, *Influx*
- Todd Defren, *PR Squared*
- Chris Dorobek, *The FCW Insider*
- Alicia Dorset, *GM FastLane*
- Kevin Dugan and Richard Laermer, *The Bad Pitch Blog*
- Eric Eggertson, *Common Sense PR*
- Li Evans, *Search Marketing Gurus*
- Kyle Flaherty, *Engage in PR*
- Susan Getgood, *Marketing Roadmaps*
- Heather Green, *Blogspotting*
- Lewis Green, *Solutions to Grow Your Business*
- Karl Greenberg, *MediaPost Publications*
- Chris Heuer, *The Future of Communities*
- Sally Seville Hodge, *Marketing Profs*
- Shel Holtz, *A Shel of my Former Self*
- John Horrigan, *Pew/Internet*
- Kami Watson Huyse, *Communications Overtones*
- Shel Isreal, *Global Neighborhoods*
- Beth Kanter, *Beth's Blog*
- Rob La Gesse, *Stuffleufagus*
- Tim Leberecht, *iPlot*
- Charlene Li, *The Groundswell*
- Joe Lichtenberg, *Marketing Profs*
- Brian Lusk, *Nuts About Southwest*
- Valeria Maltoni, *Conversation Agent*
- Richard McManus, *Read/Write Web*
- Jake Matthews, *10e20*

- Brian Oberkirch, *Like It Matters*
- Lee Odden, *Online Marketing Blog*
- Janice Partyka, *GPS World*
- Jeremy Pepper, *Pop! PR Jots*
- Ike Pigott, *Occam's Razr*
- Chris Polito, *Total Telecom*
- Jeff Pulver, *The Jeff Pulver Blog*
- Aaron Reed, *SYS-CON Media*
- Laura Ries, *Origin of Brands*
- Kim Roach, *Lifehack.org*
- Frank Rose, *Epicenter*
- Jay Rosen, *Press Think*
- Hanni Ross, *Successful Blog*
- Darren Rowse, *ProBlogger*
- Steve Rubel, *Micropersuasion*
- Mike Sansome, *ConverStations*
- David Meerman Scott, *Web Ink Now*
- Doc Searl, *Linux Journal*
- Brian Solis, *PR 2.0*
- Steve Spalding, *How to Split an Atom*
- Michael A. Stelzner, *Marketing Profs*
- Amy Stodgehill, *Green Options*
- Mario Sundar, *Marketing Nirvana*
- Dan Tapscott and Anthony Williams, *Wikinomics: The Blog*
- Robb Tokatakiya, *Tokatakiya*
- Joe Wilkert, *Publishing Blog 2020*

Additional Recommended Reading

This list was compiled by Chris Abraham, Toby Bloomberg, Eric Eggertson, Susan Getgood, Kami Huyse, Ike Pigott and Geoff Livingston, via a series of Facebook messages in Julyof 2007:

Chris Anderson, *The Long Tail*
Paul Bausch, Matthew Haughey, and Meg Hourihan, *We Blog*
Rebecca Blood, *The Weblog Handbook*
Todd Defren, *PR 2.0 Essentials* (e-book)
Susannah Gardner, *Buzz Marketing with Blogs for Dummies*
James Gleick, *Faster*
Neville Hobson and Shel Holtz, *How to Do Everything with Podcasting*

Rok Hrastnik, *Unleash the Marketing & Publishing Power of RSS*
Hugh Hewett, *Blog: Understanding the Information Reformation That's Changing Your World*
Joeseph Jaffe, *Life After the Thirty Second Spot*
Avinash Kaushik, *Web Analytics: An Hour a Day*
Richard Laermer, *Punk Marketing* (with Mark Simmons) & *Full Frontal PR* (with Michael Pricinello)
Steven Levitt and Stephen Dubner, *Freakonomics*
Christopher Locke, Rick Levine, Doc Searls, and David Weinberger, *The Cluetrain Manifesto*
Christopher Locke, *Gonzo Marketing*
Mike Moran, *Search Engine Marketing*
Katie Paine, *Measuring Success* (free e-Book)
Robert Scoble and Shel Israel, *Naked Conversations*
David Meerman Scott, *The New Rules of Marketing & PR*
Aliza Sherman, *The Everything Blogging Book*
Biz Stone, *Blogging: Genius Strategies For Instant Web Content*
Todd Stauffer, *Blog On: Building Online Communities With Web Logs*
Bob Walsh, *Clear Blogging*
Andy Wibbles, *Blogwild*
Don Tapscott and Anthony Williams, *Wikinomics*
Debbie Weil, *The Corporate Blogging Book*
Ian H. Witten, Marco Gori, and Teresa Numerico, *Web Dragons: Inside the Myths of Search Engine Technology*
Jeremy Wright, *Blog Marketing*